YONDE KAITE

よんでかいて

JAPANESE WORKBOOK

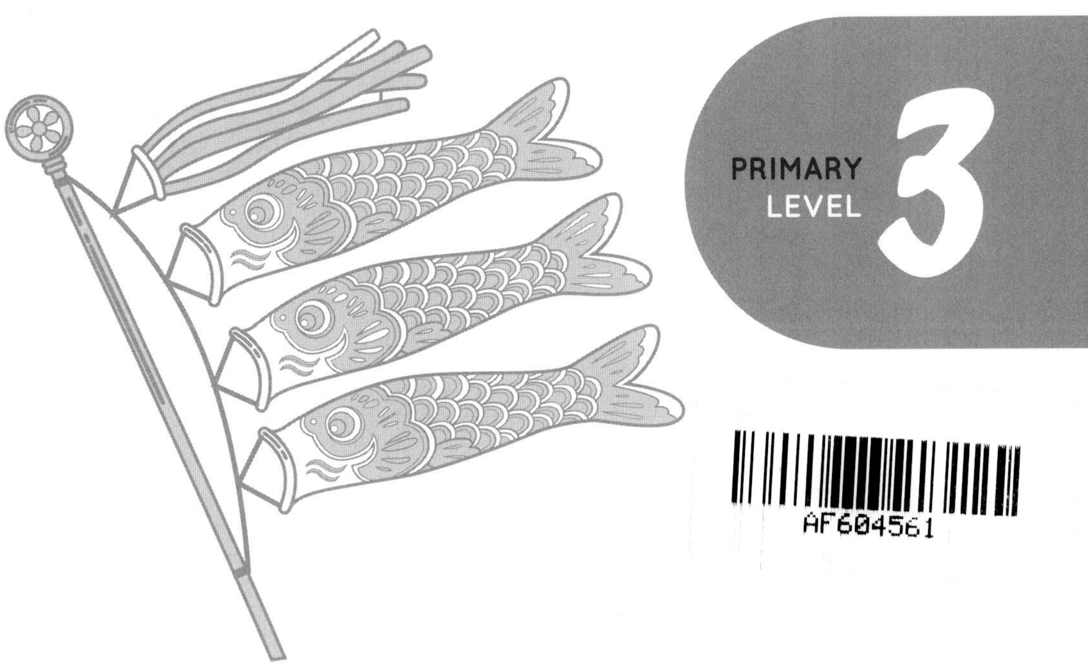

WRITTEN BY

ANNE RAJAKUMAR

WITH ORIGINAL ILLUSTRATIONS BY

JENNIFER CHENG

First published in 1998, reprinted in 2000, 2003, 2004, 2007, 2008, 2010, 2012, 2013, 2014, 2015
This redesigned edition first published in 2017, reprinted in 2019, 2020, 2022, 2023, 2025.

Insight Publications Pty Ltd
3/350 Charman Road
Cheltenham Victoria 3192
Australia

Tel: +61 3 8571 4950
Email: books@insightpublications.com.au

www.insightpublications.com.au

ISBN: 9781875882182

Illustrations by Jennifer Cheng; other images courtesy of Shutterstock
Cover and internal design by Gisela Beer
Proofing by Sage Napthine-Morrison and Fabrice Wilmann

Printed by Markono Print Media Pte Ltd

Author acknowledgements
Special thanks to my family, Kumar, Timothy and Jessica, for their constant support and assistance and to Barbara and Chris for their untiring advice and unwavering encouragement and help.

Table of Contents

日本語

ぼく は ☺☺☺ です。	I am ☺☺☺. (used by boys)
わたし は ☺☺☺ です。	I am ☺☺☺. (used by girls)
☺☺☺ さい です。	I am ☺☺☺ years old.
☺☺☺ ねんせい です。	I am in grade ☺☺☺.
こんにちは	hello

一	1	二	2	三	3	四	4	五	5	六	6	七	7	八	8	九	9	十	10

Draw a picture of yourself, then trace over the hiragana letters and complete the speech bubble. Trace over わたし は if you are a girl, and ぼく は if you are a boy. Write your name using katakana letters.

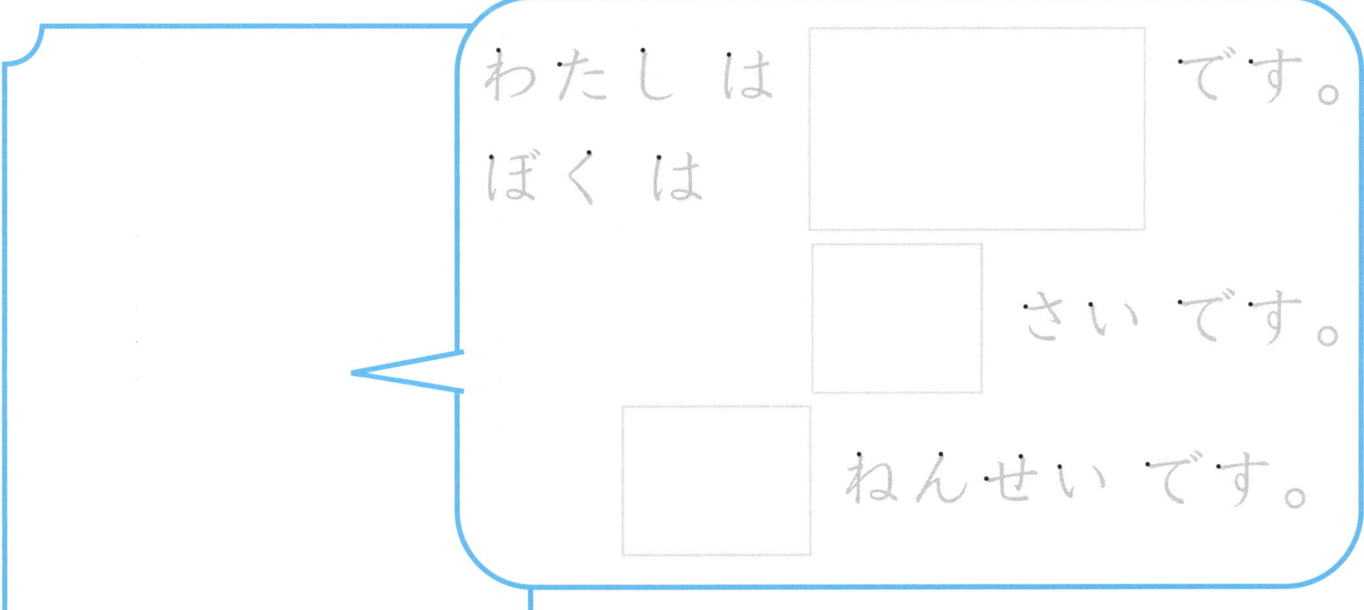

How many times can you write your name using katakana letters in this square?

I wrote my name using katakana letters ______ times.

ぼく は ☺☺☺ です。	I am ☺☺☺. (used by boys)
わたし は ☺☺☺ です。	I am ☺☺☺. (used by girls)
☺☺☺ さい です。	I am ☺☺☺ years old.
☺☺☺ ねんせい です。	I am in grade ☺☺☺.
こんにちは	hello

一	1	二	2	三	3	四	4	五	5	六	6	七	7	八	8	九	9	十	10

Trace over the Japanese letters, then answer the questions in English. There are spaces in the Japanese sentences to make them easier to read.

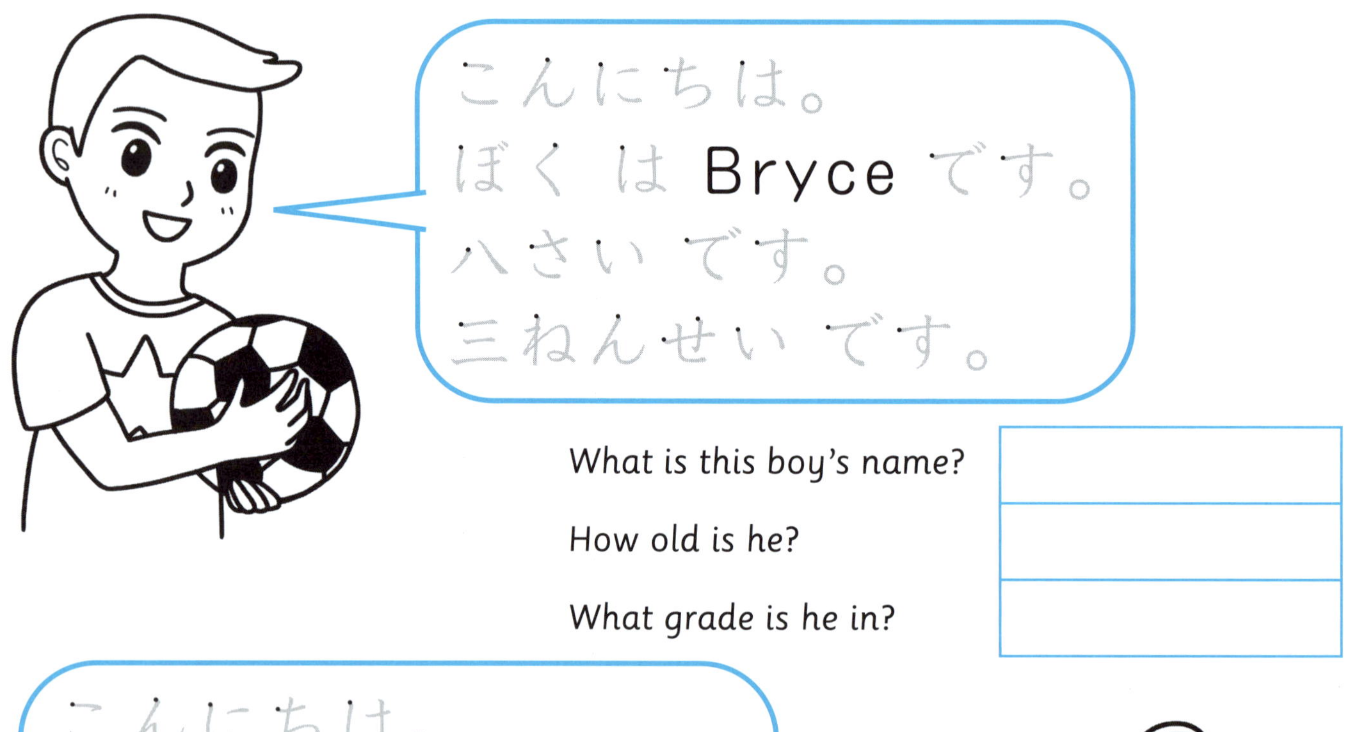

What is this boy's name? ______

How old is he? ______

What grade is he in? ______

こんにちは。
わたし は Kara です。
七さい です。
二ねんせい です。

What is this girl's name? ______

How old is she? ______

What grade is she in? ______

Trace over the Japanese place names.

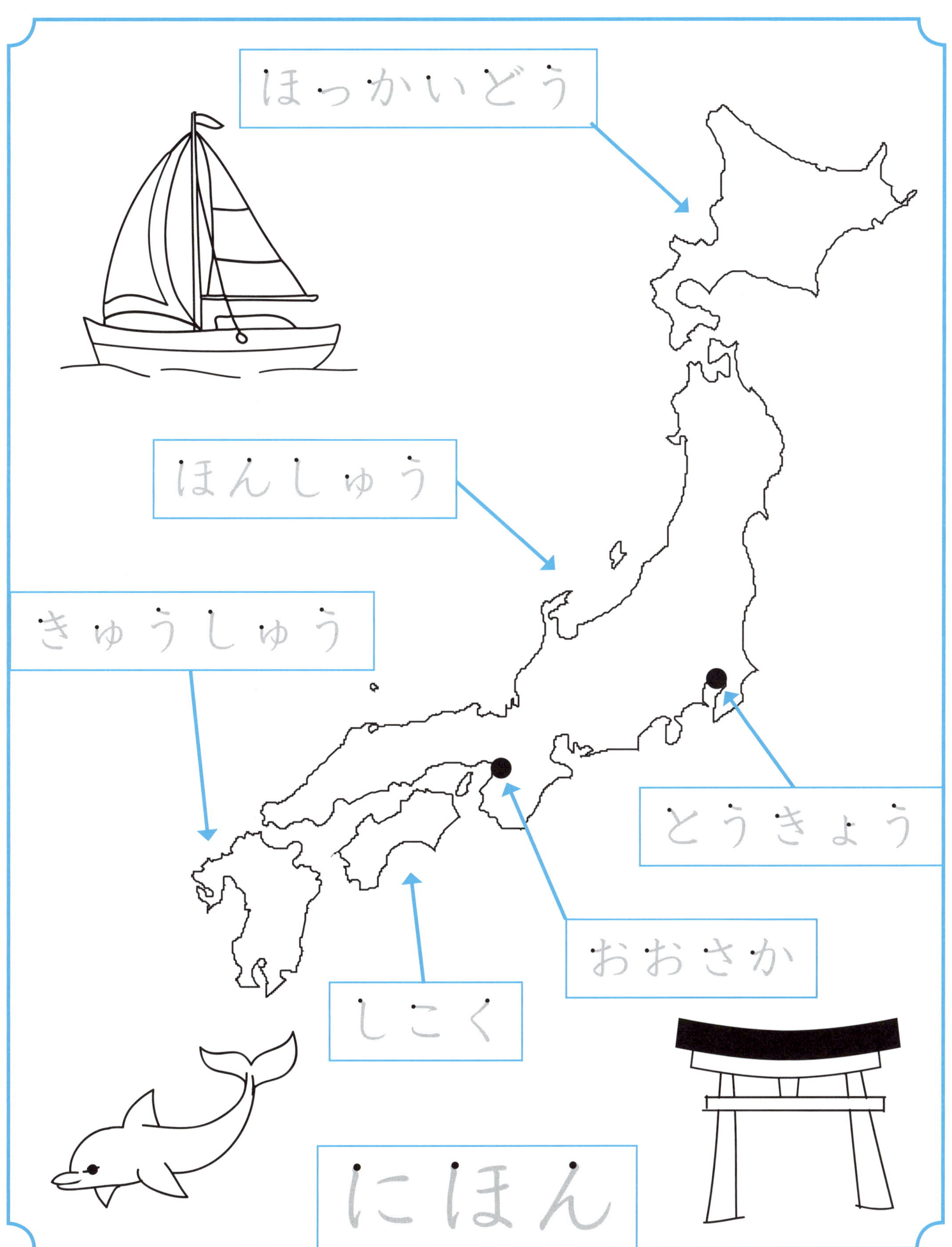

Trace over the hiragana letters, fill in the missing romaji, then join the matching names.

HONSHU

き	ゅ	う	し	ゅ	う
KYU			SHU		

JAPAN

ほ	っ	か	い	ど	う
HO	K	KA		DO	U

TOKYO

に	ほ	ん
NI	HO	

KYUSHU

し	こ	く

HOKKAIDO

と	う	き	ょ	う
	U	KYO		U

SHIKOKU

お	お	さ	か
O	O		KA

OSAKA

ほ	ん	し	ゅ	う
HO		SHU		

ぼく は ☺☺☺ です。	I am ☺☺☺. (used by boys)
わたし は ☺☺☺ です。	I am ☺☺☺. (used by girls)
くん	used after a boy's name
さん	used after a girl's name
こんにちは	hello

Look at the conversation. Trace over the hiragana letters and answer the questions.

ぼく は Bryce です。

Bryce くん、こんにちは。

わたし は Kara です。

Kara さん、こんにちは。

ぼく は Sean です。

Sean くん、こんにちは。

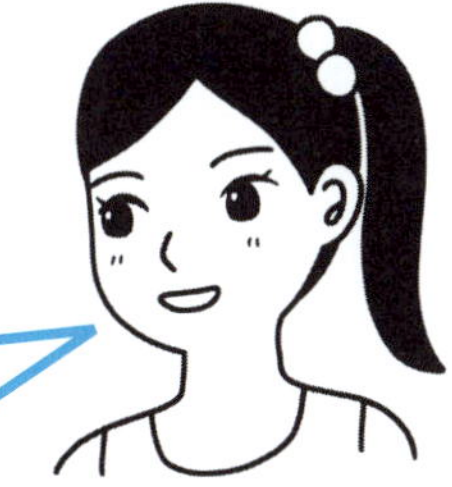

What do we say after girls' names?

What do we say after boys' names?

ぼく は ☺☺☺ です。	I am ☺☺☺. (used by boys)
わたし は ☺☺☺ です。	I am ☺☺☺. (used by girls)
くん	used after a boy's name
さん	used after a girl's name
こんにちは	hello

Trace over the hiragana letters, then fill in the missing words to complete the conversations.

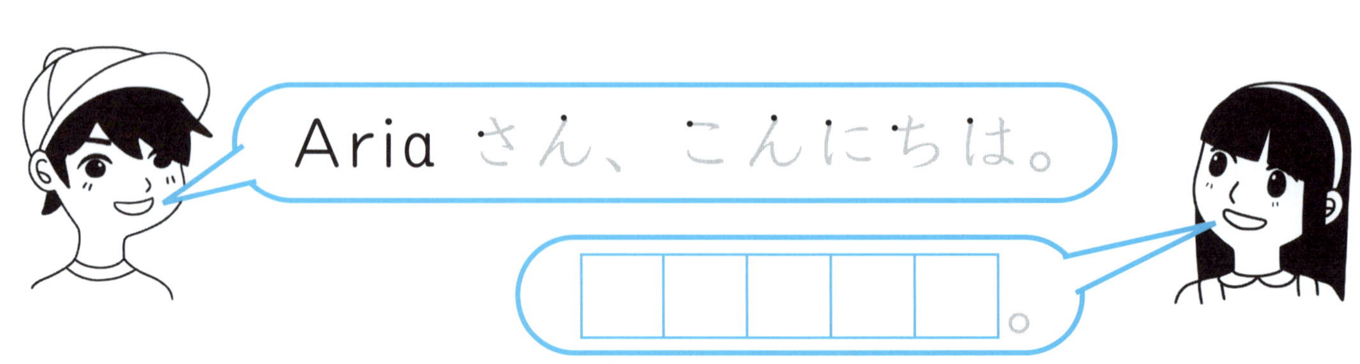

20	二	x	十	=	二	十
30	三	x	十	=	三	十
40	四	x	十	=	四	十
50	五	x	十	=	五	十
60	六	x	十	=	六	十
70	七	x	十	=	七	十
80	八	x	十	=	八	十
90	九	x	十	=	九	十

Do you remember the numbers from 1 – 10? You can use these numbers to write all the numbers up to 99. Let's practise them again. Trace over the numbers, then write them yourself in the blank boxes.

一	二	三	四	五	六	七	八	九	十

二	十	20	四	十	40	六	十	60	八	十	80
三	十	30	五	十	50	七	十	70	九	十	90

Trace over the Japanese numbers, then write the matching English numbers underneath.

四十

三十

二十

九十

二十

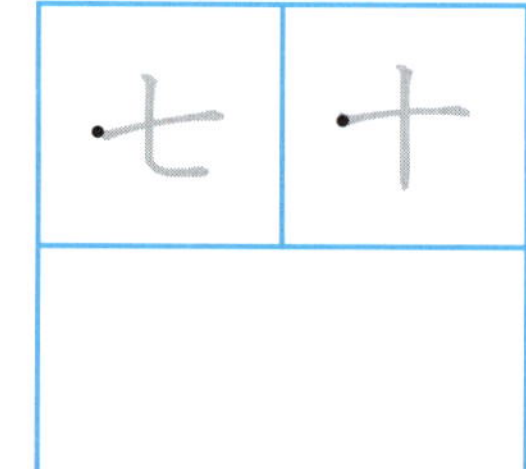

九十

五十

六十

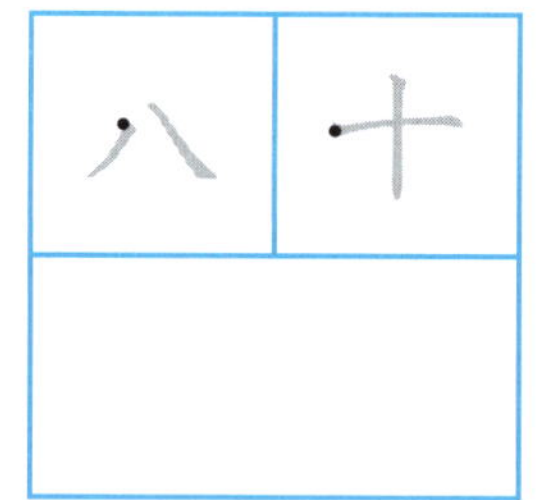

四十

三十

七十

五十

六十

21	二	x	十	+	一	=	二	十	一
22	二	x	十	+	二	=	二	十	二
23	二	x	十	+	三	=	二	十	三
24	二	x	十	+	四	=	二	十	四
25	二	x	十	+	五	=	二	十	五
26	二	x	十	+	六	=	二	十	六
27	二	x	十	+	七	=	二	十	七
28	二	x	十	+	八	=	二	十	八
29	二	x	十	+	九	=	二	十	九
30	三	x	十			=	三	十	

Write the matching English number next to the Japanese number.

二十三		二十四		三十	
二十一		二十五		二十八	
二十六		二十九		二十二	

一	1
二	2
三	3
四	4
五	5
六	6

七		7
八		8
九		9
十		10
十	一	11
十	二	12

十	三	13
十	四	14
十	五	15
十	六	16
十	七	17
十	八	18

十	九		19
二	十		20
二	十	一	21
二	十	二	22
二	十	三	23
二	十	四	24

二	十	五	25
二	十	六	26
二	十	七	27
二	十	八	28
二	十	九	29
三	十		30

Trace over the numbers, then answer the sums in Japanese.

八 + 二 = ☐

二 + 六 = ☐

三 + 二 = ☐

十 + 八 = ☐☐

九 + 七 = ☐☐

八 + 三 = ☐☐

九 + 六 = ☐☐

十二 + 六 = ☐☐

二十 + 七 = ☐☐☐

九 – 三 = ☐

十 – 五 = ☐

七 – 三 = ☐

八 + 四 = ☐☐

四 + 九 = ☐☐

十 + 五 = ☐☐

八 + 八 = ☐☐

十六 + 四 = ☐☐

十五 + 八 = ☐☐☐

あか	red
あお	blue
きいろ	yellow
しろ	white

くろ	black
みどり	green
むらさき	purple

ちゃいろ	brown
オレンジ	orange
グレー	grey
ピンク	pink

Colour the flowers in the correct colours.

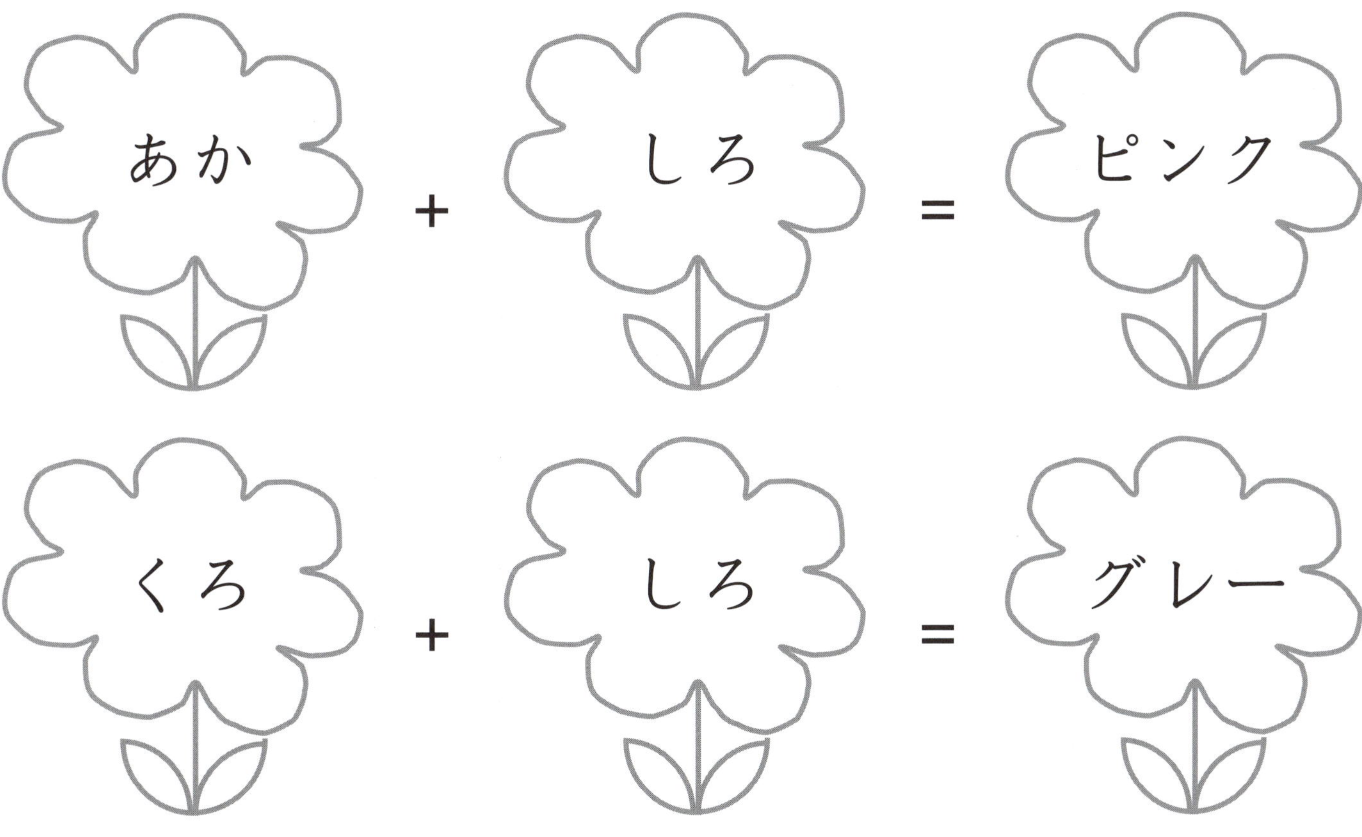

Colour the words in the correct colours.

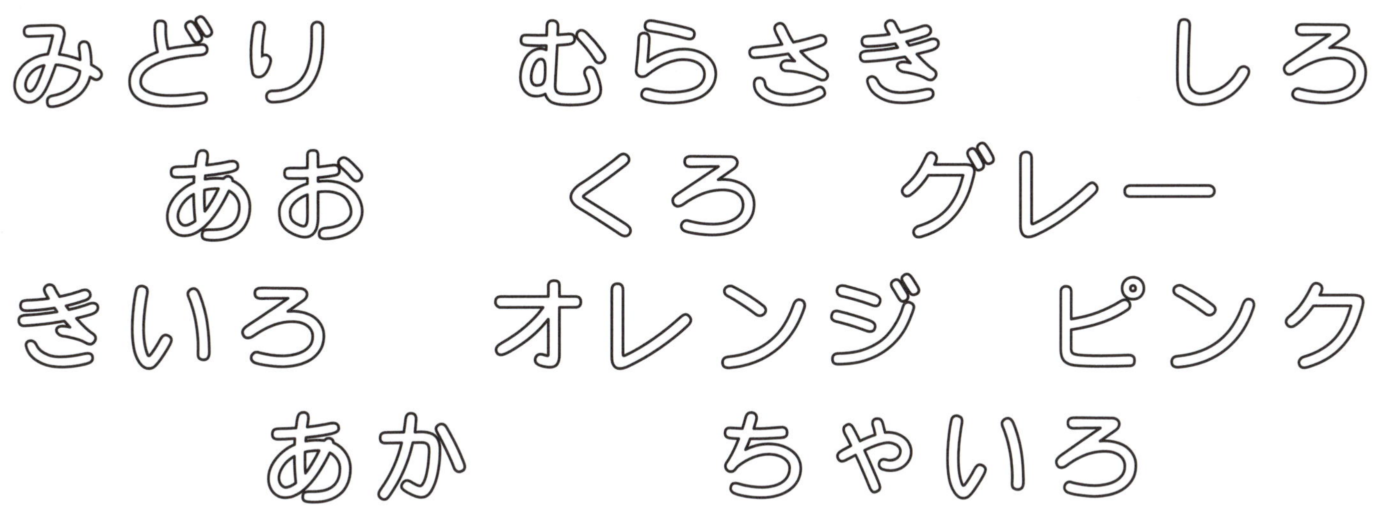

あか	red
あお	blue
きいろ	yellow
しろ	white

くろ	black
みどり	green
むらさき	purple

ちゃいろ	brown
オレンジ	orange
グレー	grey
ピンク	pink

Find and trace over the colour words in the correct colours.

そ	ち	ゃ	い	ろ	か	あ
あ	か	し	ろ	は	オ	お
ピ	ン	ク	き	い	レ	さ
み	ど	り	い	い	ン	し
く	ろ	き	ろ	ろ	ジ	た
む	ら	さ	き	グ	レ	ー

Can you write these colours in Japanese? Use one box for each letter.

white		
blue		
black		

pink			
green			
grey			

yellow				
brown				
purple				

red		

orange				

Shade the colour words in the correct colours, then trace over the rest of the song.

I CAN SING A RAINBOW

にじ が うたえる

あか きいろ ピンク みどり

むらさき オレンジ と あお

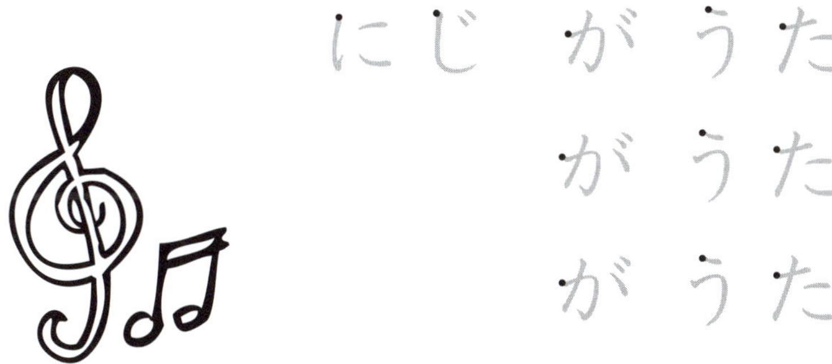

にじ が うたえる

が うたえる

が うたえる よ！

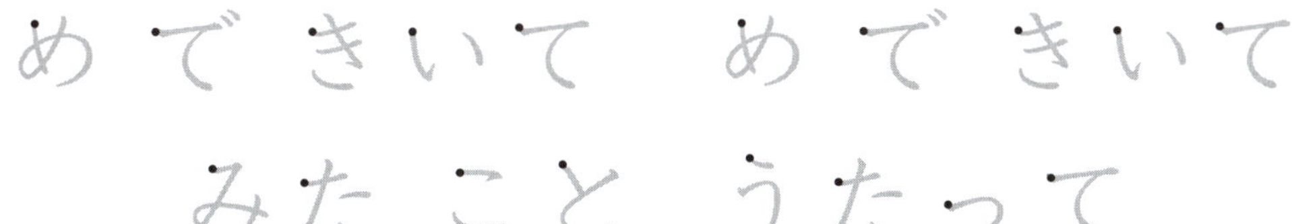

め で きいて め で きいて

みた こと うたって

にじ が うたえる

が うたえる

が うたえる よ！

あか	red
あお	blue
きいろ	yellow
しろ	white

くろ	black
みどり	green
むらさき	purple

ちゃいろ	brown
オレンジ	orange
グレー	grey
ピンク	pink

Unjumble the Japanese letters to make colour words, then write them in English.

Remember to leave a gap when you are handwriting the letters き (not き), り (not り) and さ (not さ).

JUMBLED	UNJUMBLED	ENGLISH
おあ		
ろし		
いろき		
レーグ		
クンピ		
いゃろち		
ンジオレ		
りどみ		
さむらき		
かあ		
ろく		

たべます	eat
よみます	read

みます	watch/look
べんきょう します	learn

Trace over the correct verb (doing word).

eat	たへます	たべはす	たべます	なべます
read	もみます	よみます	まみます	よみほす
look	します	みほす	みます	みまむ
learn	べんきようします	べんきょうします		

Trace over the hiragana letters, then join the verb (doing word) to the matching picture.

たべます

よみます

べんきょう します

みます

Which two hiragana letters do verbs (doing words) end in?

Hiragana:

Romaji:

たべます	eat
よみます	read

みます	watch/look
べんきょう します	learn

Collect the hiragana letters along the path, then write the words you have made in Japanese and English.

Japanese:				
English:				

サンドイッチ	sandwich
ほん	book
にほんご	Japanese
テレビ	TV

particle O
を

たべます	eat
よみます	read
べんきょうします	learn
みます	watch

Trace over, then copy the sentences. Colour particle O in your brightest colour.

Draw a picture that matches your sentence.

サンドイッチ	sandwich
ほん	book
にほんご	Japanese
テレビ	TV

particle O
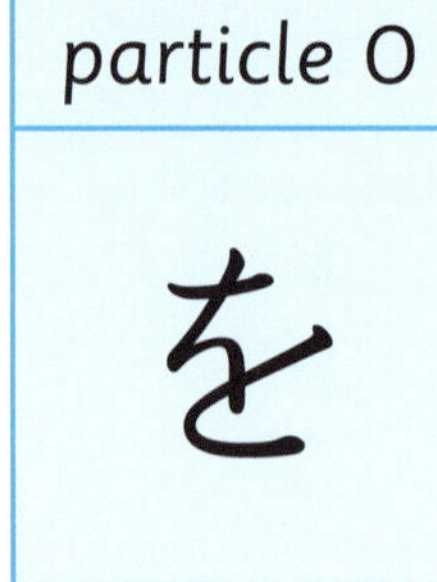

たべます	eat
よみます	read
べんきょう します	learn
みます	watch

Trace over the Japanese words, then fill in the blank boxes to complete the sentences. What does your sentence say in English? The first English sentence has been done for you. HINT: If there is no name in the Japanese sentence, start your English sentence with "I …". Don't forget to put a full stop in its own box!

サ	ン	ド	イ	ッ	チ		た	べ	ま	す	。

English: I eat sandwiches.

ほ	ん	を					

English: ______________________________

				を	べ	ん	き	ょ	う	し	ま	す	。

English: ______________________________

テ	レ	ビ	を				。

English: ______________________________

Can you remember these words in Japanese? Write your answer using hiragana or katakana letters. REMEMBER: Put one letter in each box!

Japan			

grey			

red		

watch			

hello					

blue		

	particle WA		particle O	
はな さん		サンドイッチ		たべます
Hana - san		sandwich		eat
Kara さん		ほん		よみます
Kara - san	は	book	を	read
Bryce くん		にほんご		べんきょうします
Bryce - kun		Japanese		learn
たか くん		テレビ		みます
Taka - kun		TV		watch

Colour the matching English and Japanese words in the same colour, then join them with a line. The first one has been done for you.

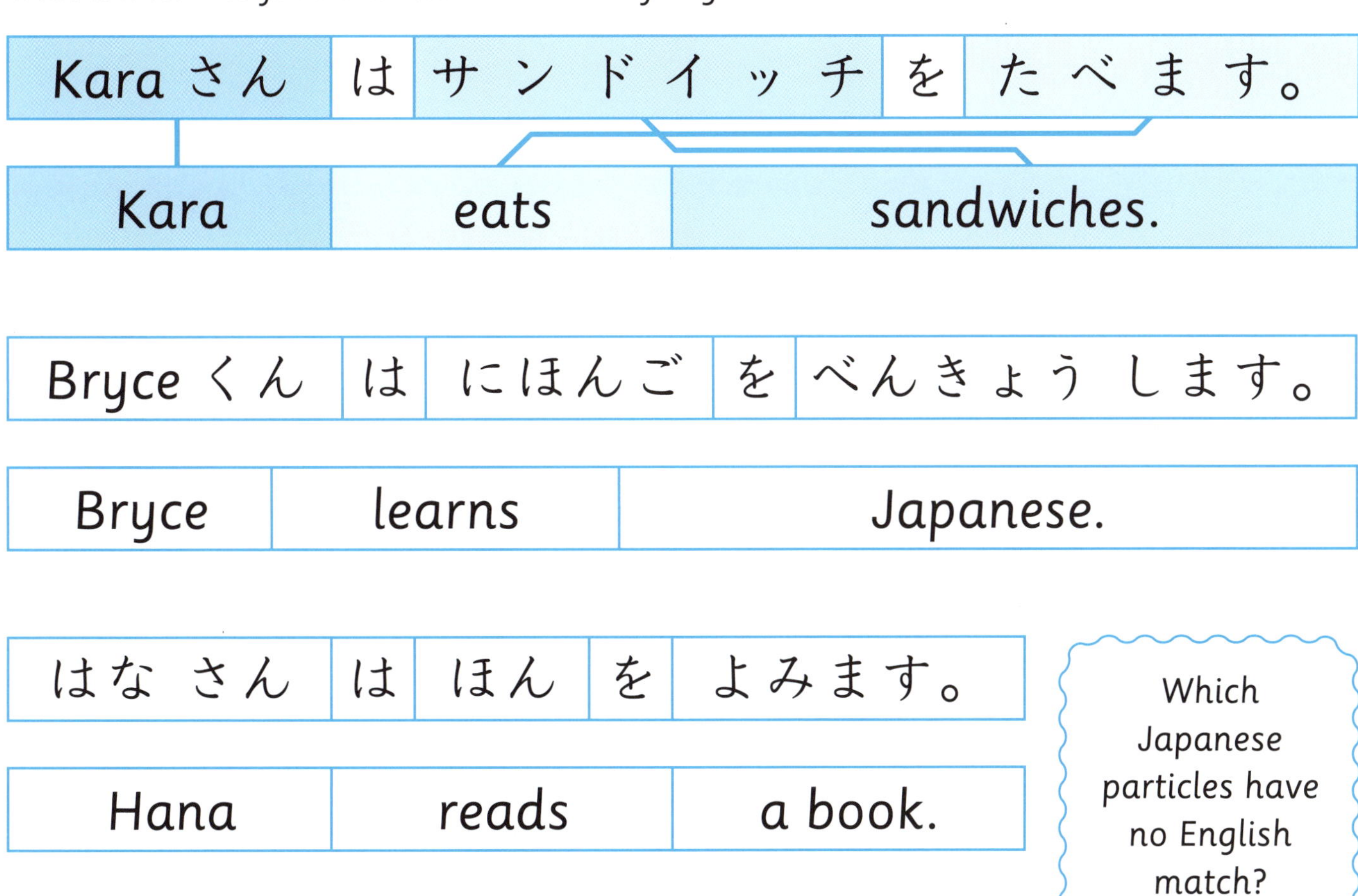

たか くん	は	テレビ	を	みます。

Taka	watches	TV.

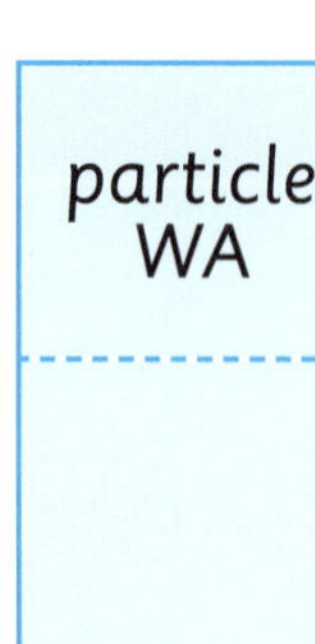
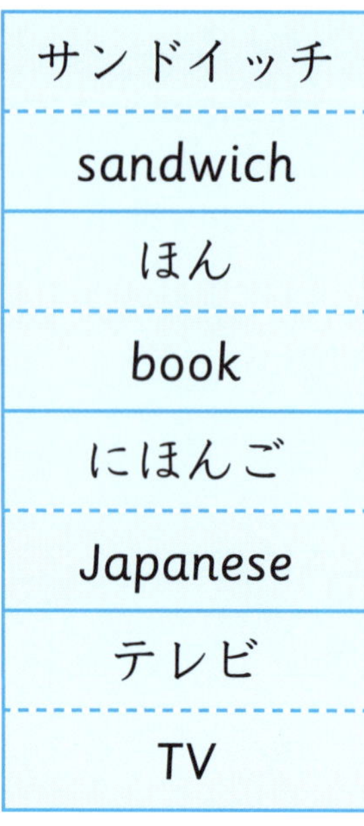

はな さん	particle WA	サンドイッチ	particle O	たべます
Hana - san		sandwich		eat
Kara さん		ほん		よみます
Kara - san		book		read
Bryce くん	は	にほんご	を	べんきょう します
Bryce - kun		Japanese		learn
たか くん		テレビ		みます
Taka - kun		TV		watch

Trace over these sentences. What do they say in English?

はな さん は テレビ を みます。

English: ______________________________

Kara さん は にほんご を べんきょう します。

English: ______________________________

Bryce くん は サンドイッチ を たべます。

English: ______________________________

Can you write this sentence in Japanese? (There's no need to leave spaces in a Japanese sentence, but don't forget the full stop at the end!)

Taka reads books.

Japanese: | | | | | | | | | | | | | |

たべます	eat	たべて ください。	Please eat.
よみます	read	よんで ください。	Please read.
みます	watch/look	みて ください。	Please watch/look.
べんきょう します	learn	べんきょう して ください。	Please learn.

Complete the crossword in Japanese. Write your answers using hiragana letters.

1. 2. 3. 4. 5. 6. 7.

Across

4. learn
5. look
6. Please eat.
7. please

Down

1. eat
2. Please learn.
3. read
5. Please look.

たべます	eat	たべて ください。	Please eat.
よみます	read	よんで ください。	Please read.
みます	watch/look	みて ください。	Please watch/look.
べんきょう します	learn	べんきょう して ください。	Please learn.

Trace over the hiragana letters, then fill in the blanks.

た		ま	す
	BE	MA	
eat			

よ	み	ま	す
YO	MI		

べ		き	ょ	う		ま	す
BE	N	KYO		U	SHI	MA	

み	ま	す
MI		
look/watch		

Trace over the Japanese words, then connect the matching sentences with a line.

べんきょう して ください。 Please look.

みて ください。 Please learn.

よんで ください。 Please eat.

たべて ください。 Please read.

サンドイッチ	sandwich
ほん	book
にほんご	Japanese
テレビ	TV

particle O
を

たべて ください。	Please eat.
よんで ください。	Please read.
みて ください。	Please watch/look.
べんきょう して ください。	Please learn.

Trace over, then copy the sentences. Colour particle を in your brightest colour. Colour ください (please) in a different colour. What do your sentences say in English?

サ	ン	ド	イ	ッ	チ	を	た	べ	て	く	だ	さ	い	。

English: ______________________________

に	ほ	ん	ご	を	べ	ん	き	ょ	う	し	て	く	だ	さ	い	。

English: ______________________________

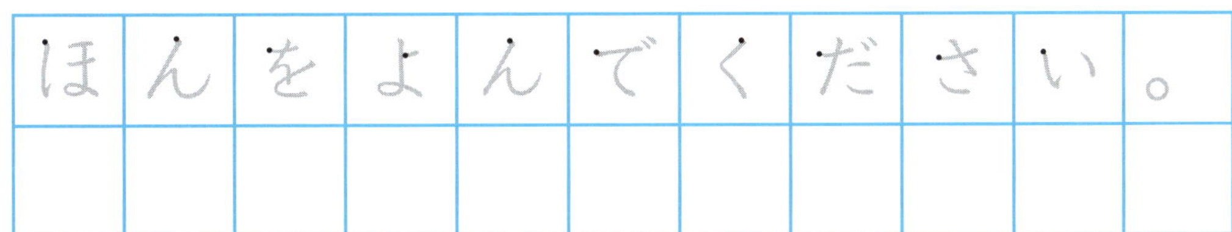

English: ______________________________

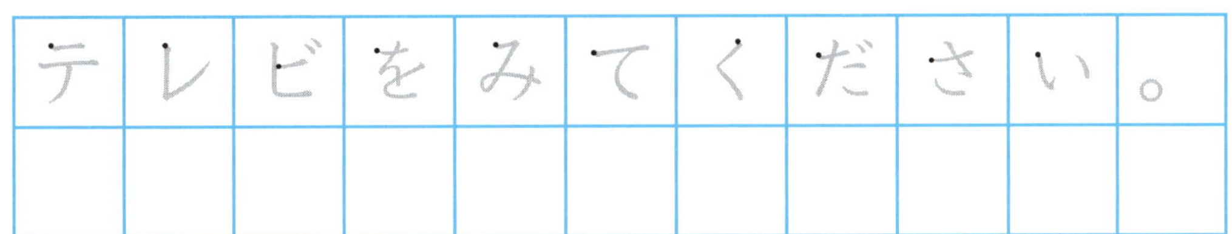

English: ______________________________

サンドイッチ	sandwich
ほん	book
にほんご	Japanese
テレビ	TV

particle O

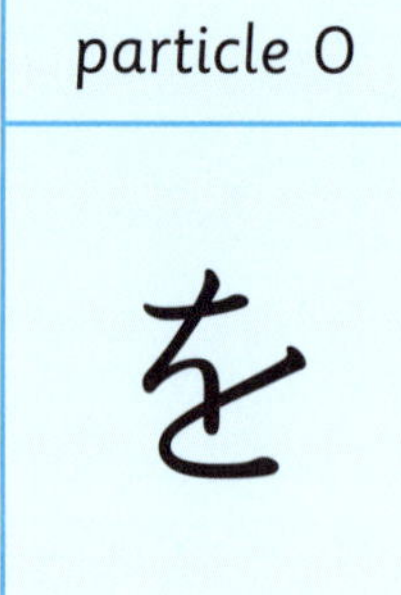

たべて ください。	Please eat.
よんで ください。	Please read.
みて ください。	Please watch/look.
べんきょう して ください。	Please learn.

Use this code to crack the mystery sentences.

1	2	3	4	5	6	7	8	9	10	11	12	13	14	15	16	17	18
。	し	い	よ	ん	ほ	う	く	て	さ	を	に	べ	ご	き	ょ	だ	で

Mystery sentence: 6 5 11 4 5 18 8 17 10 3 1

Japanese: | | | | | | | | | | | |

English: ______________________________

Mystery sentence: 12 6 5 14 11 13 5 15 16 7
2 9 8 17 10 3 1

Japanese: | | | | | | | | | | |
| | | | | | | |

English: ______________________________

Colour in the pairs if they match. Leave them blank if they do not.

よんで ください。	テレビ	サンドイッチ
Please read.	sandwich	book

みて ください。	ほん	にほんご
Please learn.	book	Japanese

一じ	1 o'clock	五じ	5 o'clock	九じ	9 o'clock
二じ	2 o'clock	六じ	6 o'clock	十じ	10 o'clock
三じ	3 o'clock	七じ	7 o'clock	十一じ	11 o'clock
四じ	4 o'clock	八じ	8 o'clock	十二じ	12 o'clock

いま なんじ です か。	What's the time?

Trace over the time words.

TELL-THE-TIME ROCK

(to the tune of 'Rock Around the Clock')

いま なんじ です か。

What's the time?

一じ 二じ 三じ rock,
四じ 五じ 六じ rock,
七じ 八じ 九じ rock,
Rock around the clock tonight!
When you add a じ that says o'clock,
一じ, 二じ it's the tell-the-time rock!

三じ 四じ 五じ rock,
六じ 七じ 八じ rock,
九じ 十じ 十一じ rock,

Now it's 十二じ, which is 12 o'clock,
And that's the end of our tell-the-time rock!

一じ	1 o'clock
二じ	2 o'clock
三じ	3 o'clock
四じ	4 o'clock

五じ	5 o'clock
六じ	6 o'clock
七じ	7 o'clock
八じ	8 o'clock

九じ	9 o'clock
十じ	10 o'clock
十一じ	11 o'clock
十二じ	12 o'clock

いま なんじ です か。	What's the time?

Draw the clock hands in the correct places.

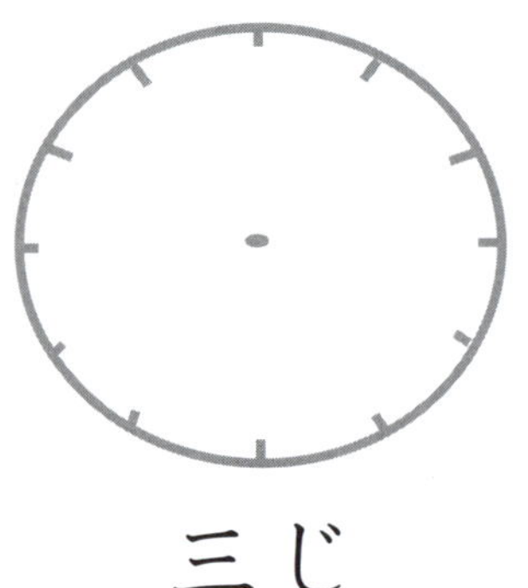

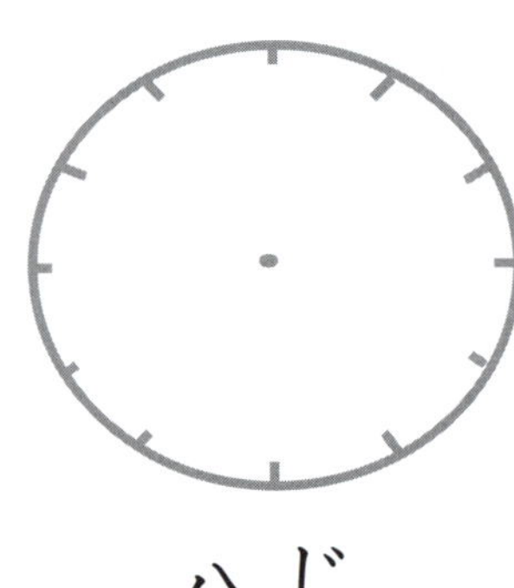

八じ

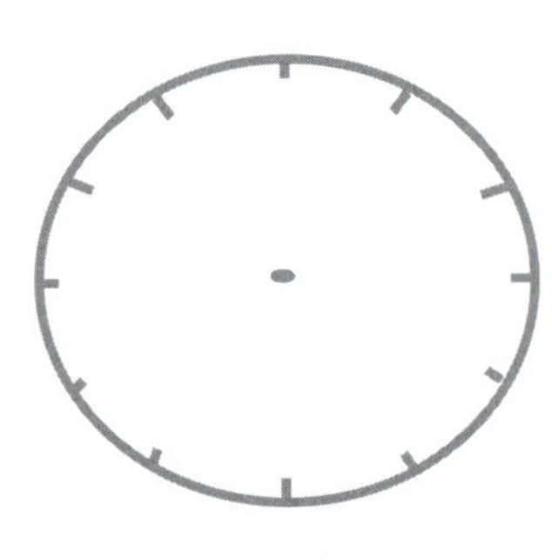

六じ

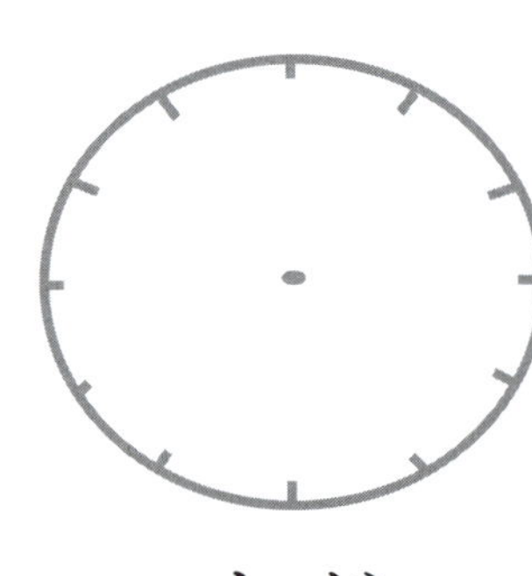

九じ

Write the time in Japanese.

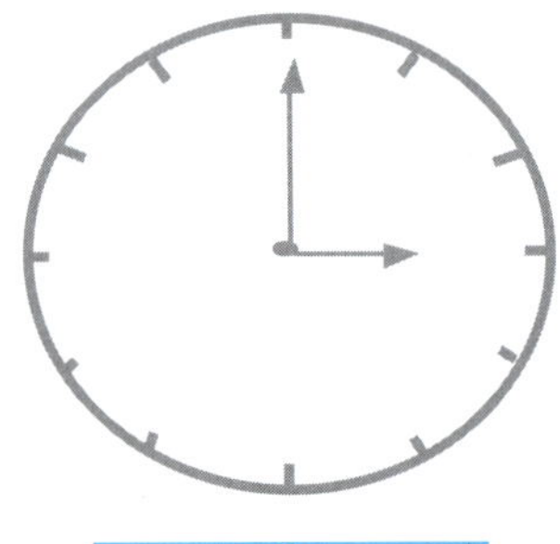

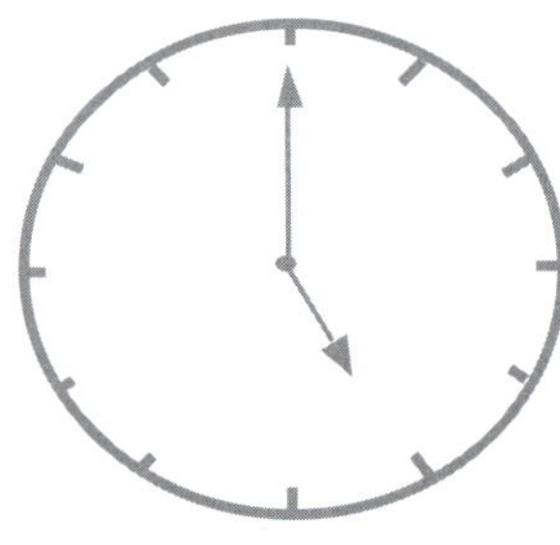

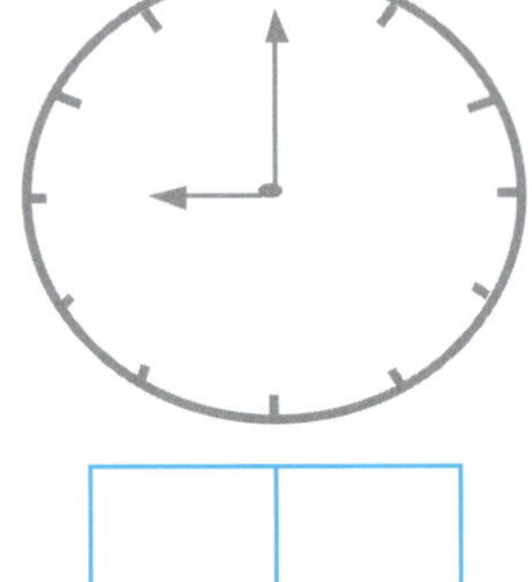

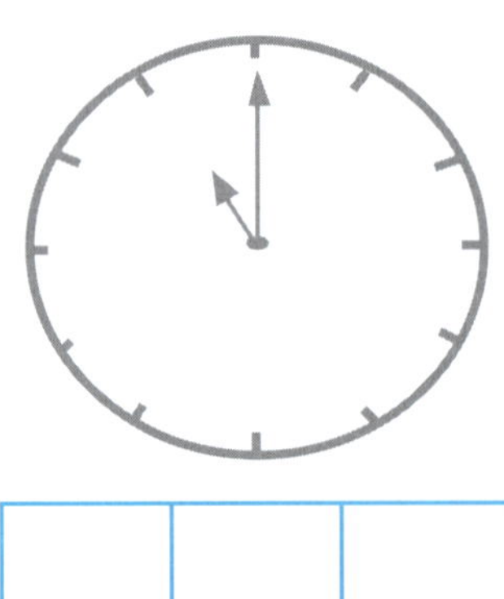

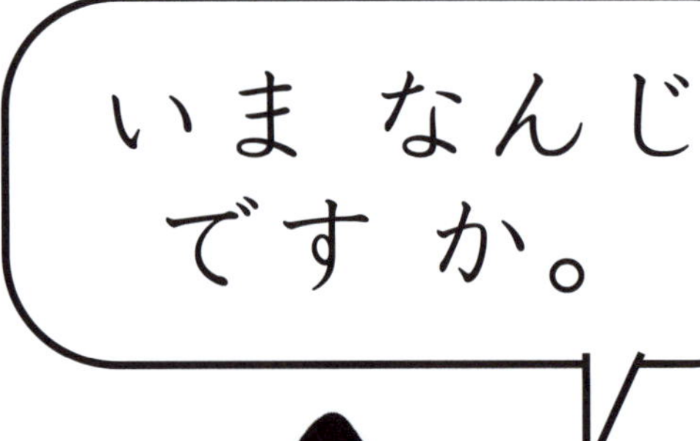

一	五	九
1	5	9
二	六	十
2	6	10
三	七	十一
3	7	11
四	八	十二
4	8	12

o'clock	particle NI (at)
じ	に

たべます
eat
よみます
read
べんきょう します
learn
みます
watch

Find and shade the verbs (doing words) in a special colour. Find and shade particle に in a different colour. Answer the questions in English (or Japanese).

四じ に べんきょう します。

When does Elijah learn?

____

What does Aria do at 2 o'clock?

____

When does Taka eat?

____

How do we write particle に in romaji?

一	五	九
1	5	9
二	六	十
2	6	10
三	七	十一
3	7	11
四	八	十二
4	8	12

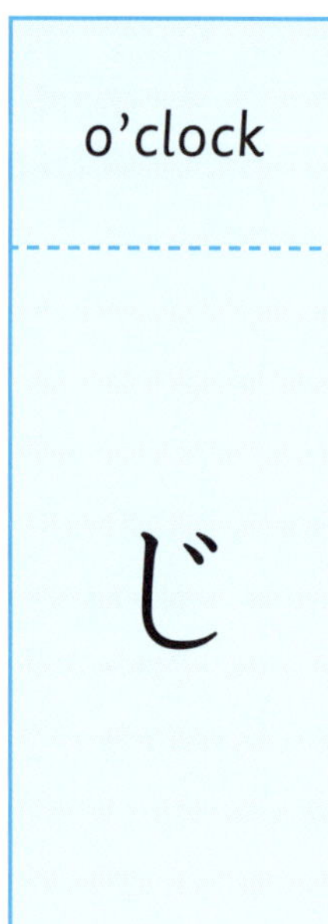

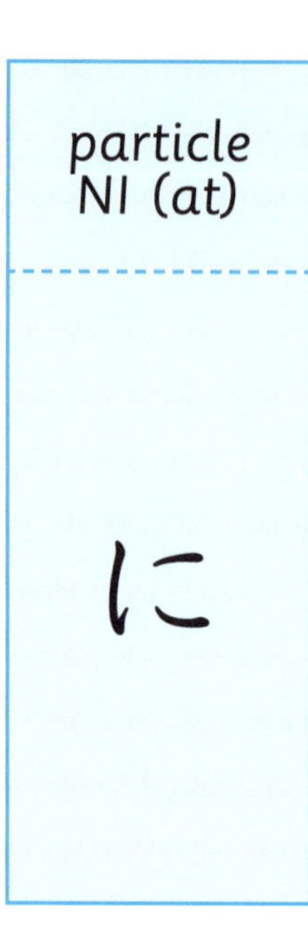

たべます
eat
よみます
read
べんきょう します
learn
みます
watch

Put the Japanese words in the correct order to make a sentence, then write your new sentence in English. The first one has been done for you to trace over. Remember not to leave spaces between your words!

Japanese words	に たべます 十一じ 。								
Japanese sentence	十	一	じ	に	た	べ	ま	す	。

English: I eat at 11 o'clock.

Japanese words	。 よみます に 三じ							
Japanese sentence								

English: ______________________

Japanese words	べんきょう します 。 に 六じ											
Japanese sentence												

English: ______________________

Japanese words	みます 。 に 八じ						
Japanese sentence							

English: ______________________

一	五	九
1	5	9
二	六	十
2	6	10
三	七	十一
3	7	11
四	八	十二
4	8	12

o'clock

particle NI (at)

サンドイッチ	sandwich
ほん	book
にほんご	Japanese
テレビ	TV

particle O

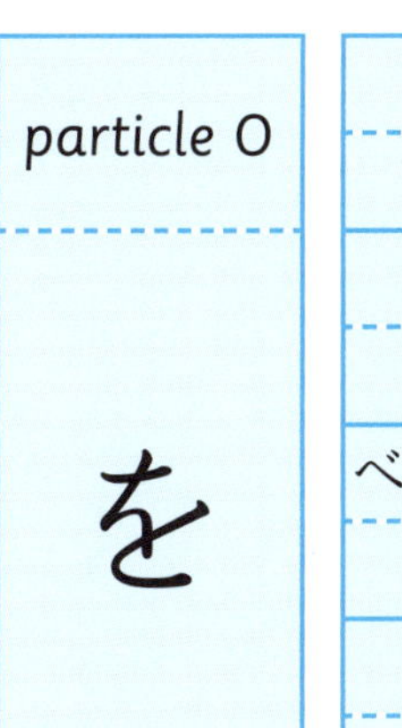

たべます	eat
よみます	read
べんきょうします	learn
みます	watch

Trace over the hiragana letters, then fill in the missing particles in the shaded boxes. Can you answer the questions in English? Have a go!

When do I read a book? ______________________________

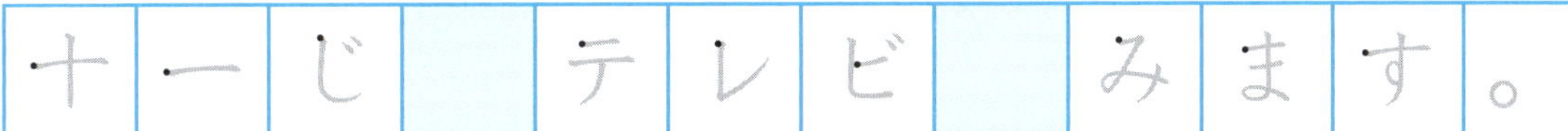

What do I do at 11 o'clock? ______________________________

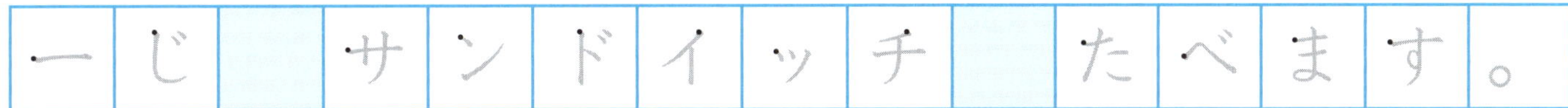

When do I eat a sandwich? ______________________________

What do I do at five o'clock? ______________________________

Circle the three differences between the particle O on the left and the one on the right. Then write it correctly in the blank box.

一	五	九	o'clock	particle NI (at)	サンドイッチ	particle O	たべます
1	5	9			sandwich		eat
二	六	十			ほん		よみます
2	6	10			book		read
三	七	十一	じ	に	にほんご	を	べんきょう します
3	7	11			Japanese		learn
四	八	十二			テレビ		みます
4	8	12			TV		watch

ぼく は ☺☺☺ です。	I am ☺☺☺. (used by boys)
わたし は ☺☺☺ です。	I am ☺☺☺. (used by girls)
☺☺☺ さい です。	I am ☺☺☺ years old.
☺☺☺ ねんせい です。	I am in grade ☺☺☺.
こんにちは	hello

Trace over the Japanese sentences in the speech box, then answer the questions in English or Japanese.

こんにちは。
ぼく は Sean です。 六さい です。
三ねんせい です。
七じ に ほん を よみます。
六じ に たべます。
四じ に テレビ を みます。
二じ に にほんご を べんきょう します。

What is this boy's name? ______________________________

How old is he? ______________________________

What grade is he in? ______________________________

When does he eat? ______________________________

What does he do at 7 o'clock? ______________________________

When does he learn Japanese? ______________________________

たか	Taka (a boy's name)
くん	used after boys' names
は	particle WA
みます	watches/looks

テレビ	TV
を	particle O
五じ	5 o'clock
に	particle NI (at)

Trace over the sentence as it becomes longer and longer. Highlight the matching English and Japanese words in the same colour. Highlight the particles in a special colour.

たか くん

Taka

たか くん は みます。

Taka watches.

たか くん は テレビ を みます。

Taka watches TV.

たか くん は 五じ に テレビ を みます。

Taka watches TV at 5 o'clock.

はな	Hana (a girl's name)
さん	used after girls' names
は	particle WA
よみます	read

ほん	book
を	particle O
八じ	8 o'clock
に	particle NI (at)

Trace over the sentence as it becomes longer and longer. Can you fill in the missing words or particles?

はな＿＿

Hana

Hana reads.

はなさんは＿＿をよみます。

Hana reads a book.

Hana reads a book at 5 o'clock.

Can you make some long sentences of your own? Use as many squares for your Japanese sentence as you need and leave the rest blank. Then write it in English underneath.

Japanese:

English: ______________________

____

Japanese:

English: ______________________

____

A	一	ナ	あ	あ	あ	あ	あ
I	い	い	い	い	い	い	い
U	`	う	う	う	う	う	う
E	`	え	え	え	え	え	え
O	一	お	お	お	お	お	お

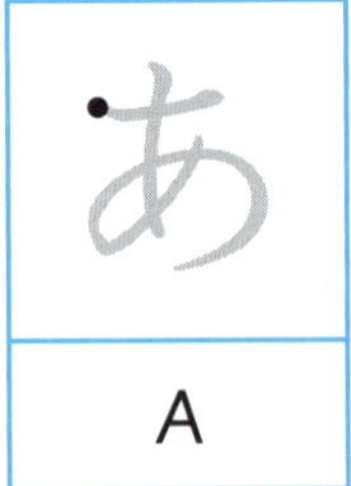

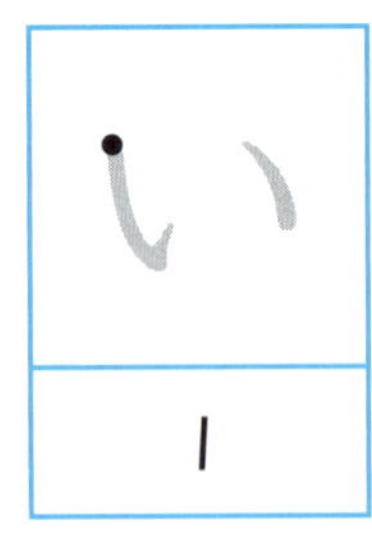

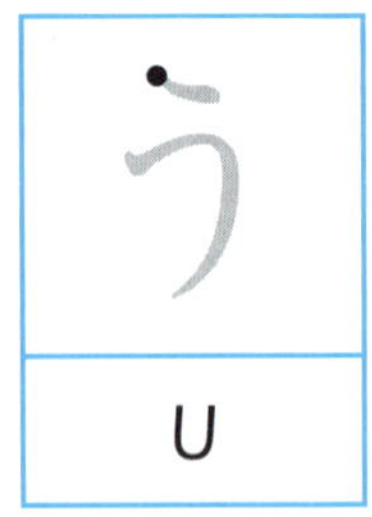

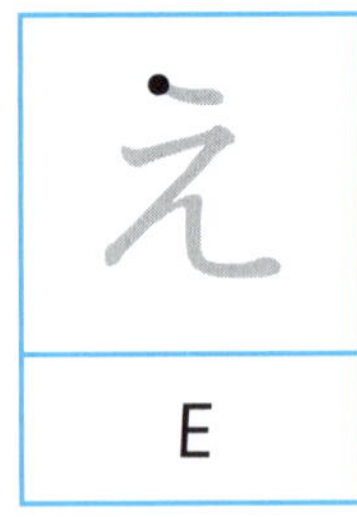

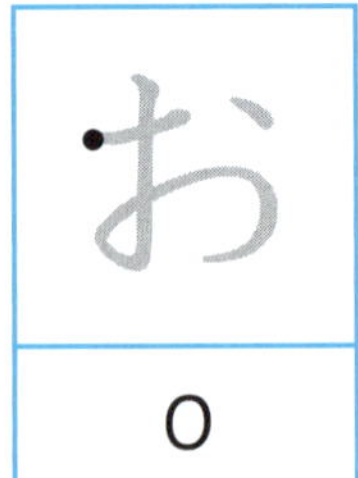

Fill in the missing hiragana letters to complete the labels.

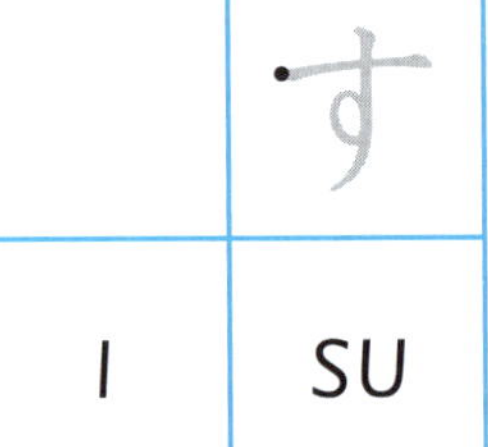

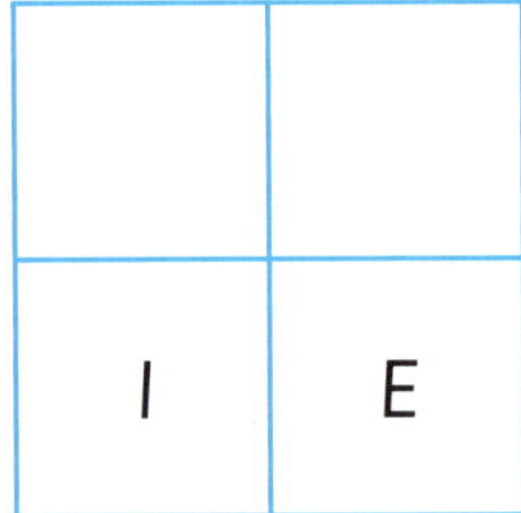

	か	ち	ゃ	ん
A	KA	CHA		N

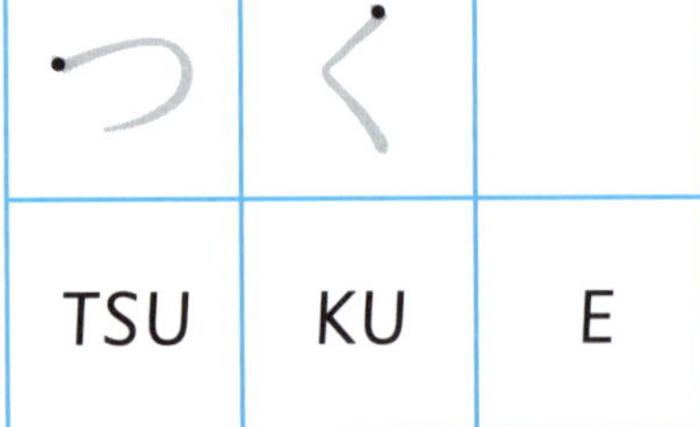

	し
U	SHI

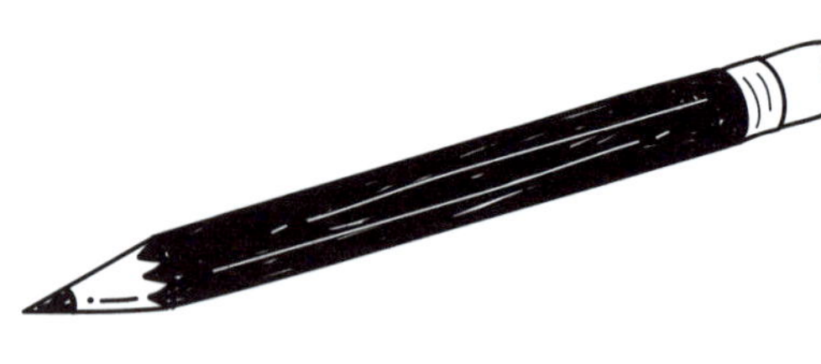

	ん	ぴ	つ
E	N	PI	TSU

KA			か	か	か	か	か
✍							
KI				き	き	き	き
✍							
KU	く	く	く	く	く	く	く
✍							
KE			け	け	け	け	け
✍							
KO		こ	こ	こ	こ	こ	こ
✍							

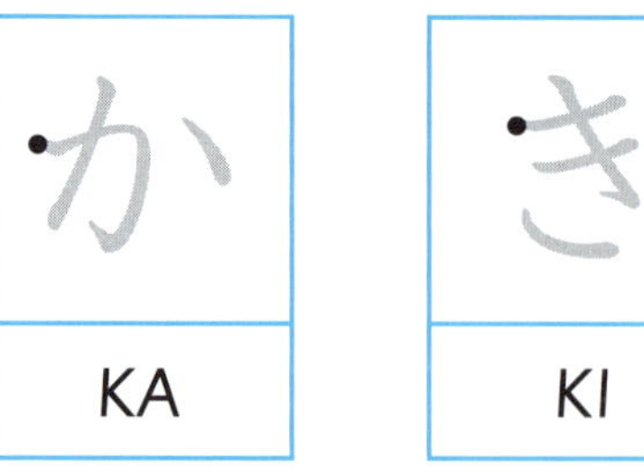
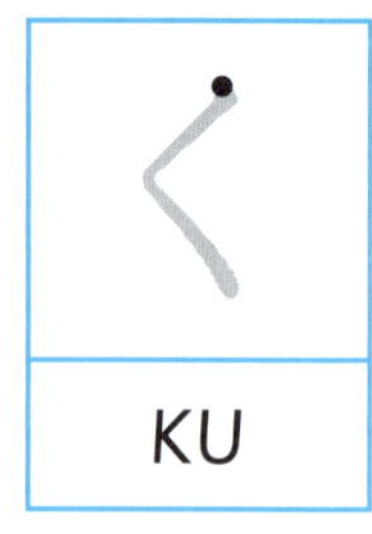
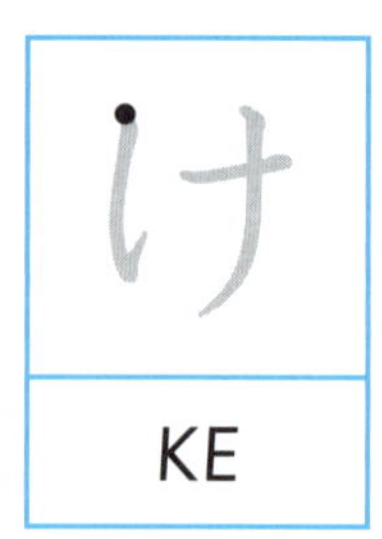
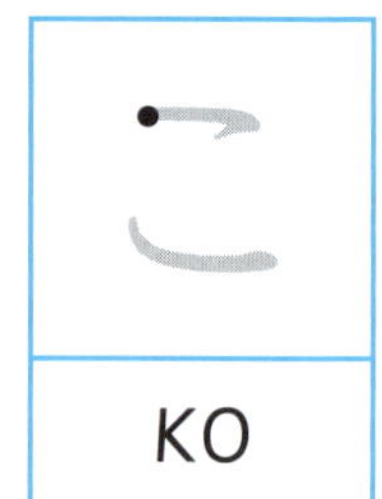

か	き	く	け	こ
KA	KI	KU	KE	KO

Help the Japanese schoolboy get to school. Trace over the hiragana letters along the correct path. How many of each hiragana letter did he find along the way?

KA		KI		KU		KE		KO	

SA	一	さ	さ	さ	さ	さ	さ
SHI	し	し	し	し	し	し	し
SU	一	す	す	す	す	す	す
SE	一	十	せ	せ	せ	せ	せ
SO	そ	そ	そ	そ	そ	そ	そ

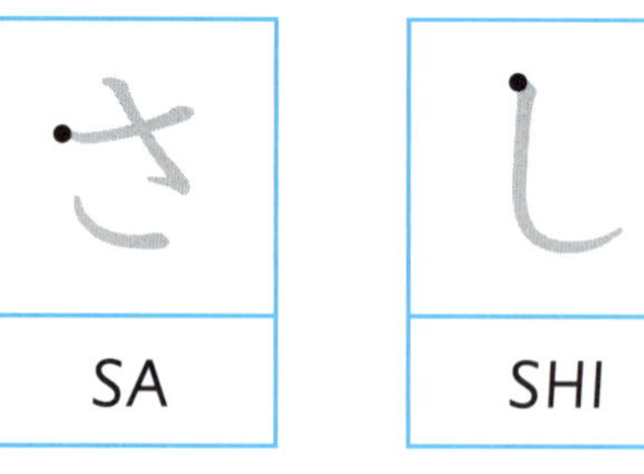
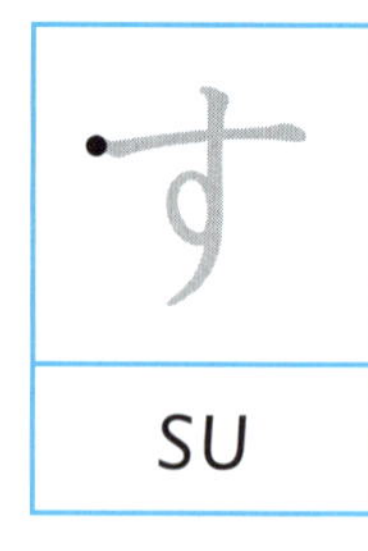
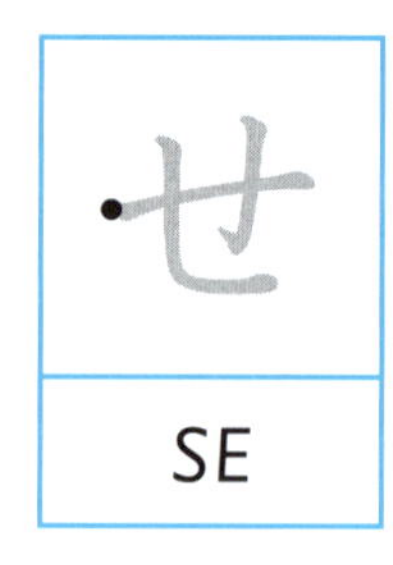
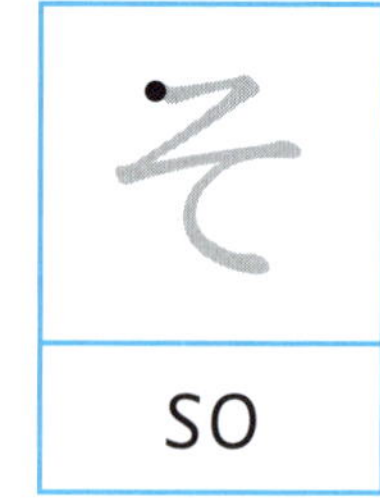

さ	し	す	せ	そ
SA	SHI	SU	SE	SO

Fill in the missing hiragana letters to complete the sentences.

I am Hana.

わ	た		は	は		で		。
WA	TA	SHI	WA	HA	NA	DE	SU	.

Hello.

	ん	に	ち	は	。
KO	N	NI	CHI	WA	.

I'm 8 years old.

は	っ			で		。
HA	S	SA	I	DE	SU	.

I'm in grade 3.

	ん	ね	ん			で		。
SA	N	NE	N	SE	I	DE	SU	.

TA				た	た	た	た
CHI		ち	ち	ち	ち	ち	ち
TSU	つ	つ	つ	つ	つ	つ	つ
TE	て	て	て	て	て	て	て
TO		と	と	と	と	と	と

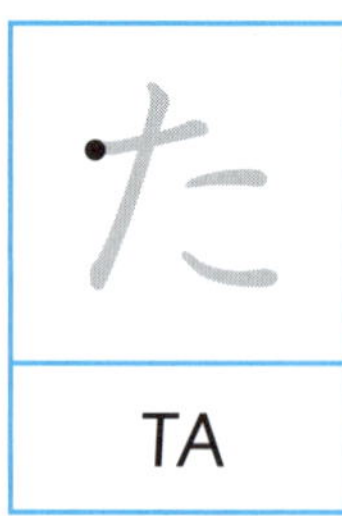

TA

CHI

TSU

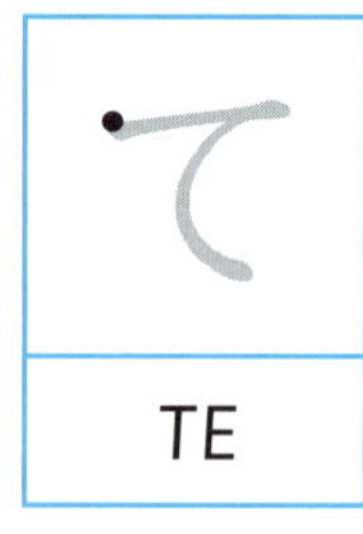

TE

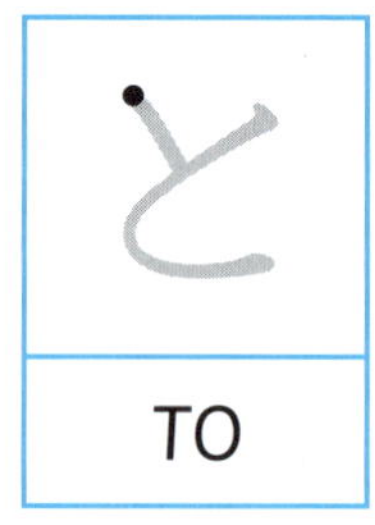

TO

Trace over the small hiragana letters to make large hiragana letters. Which letters have you made? Write your answers in romaji.

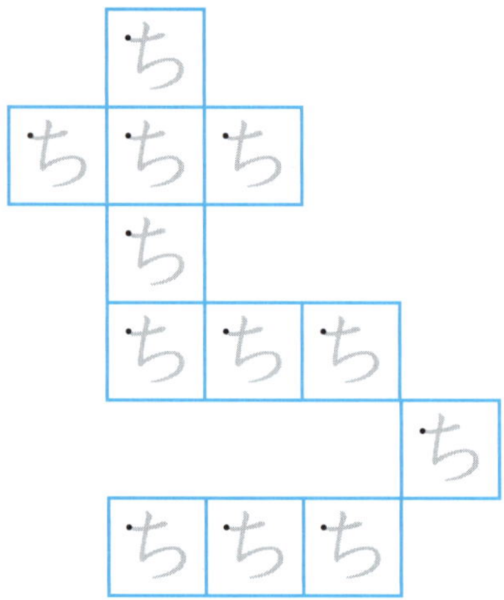

I made the letter: ____________________

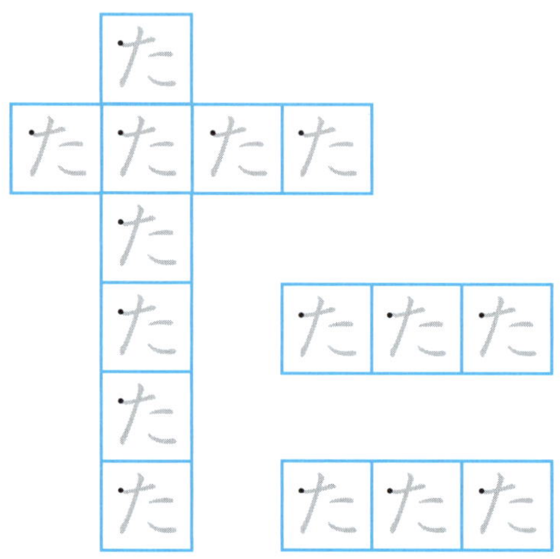

I made the letter: ____________________

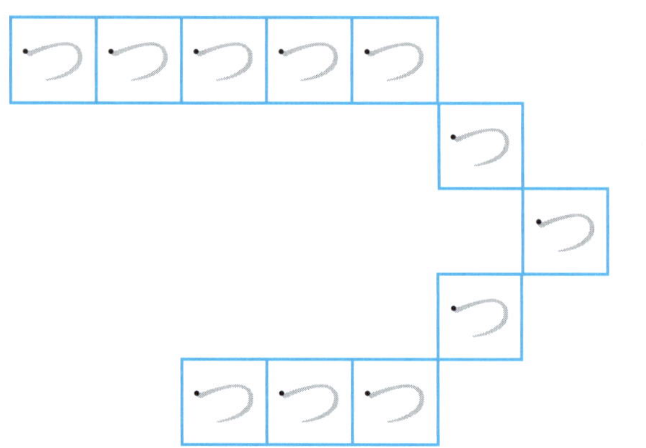

I made the letter: ____________________

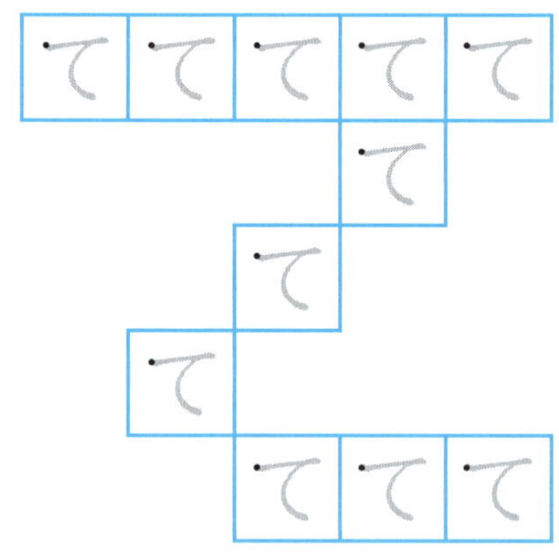

I made the letter: ____________________

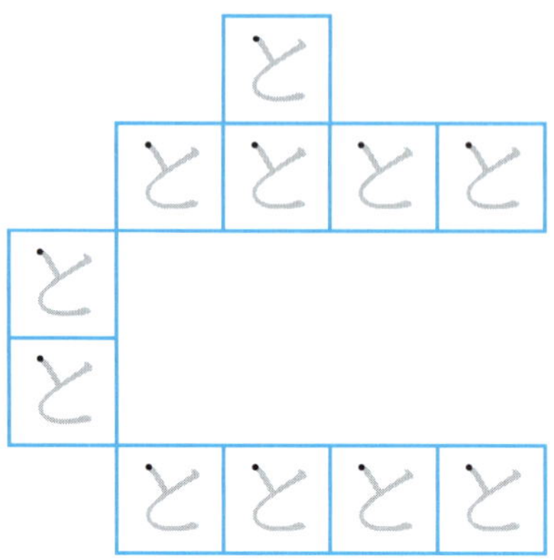

I made the letter: ____________________

NA	ー	ナ	ナ	な	な	な	な
NI	l	に	に	に	に	に	に
NU	ヽ	ぬ	ぬ	ぬ	ぬ	ぬ	ぬ
NE	l	ね	ね	ね	ね	ね	ね
NO	の	の	の	の	の	の	の

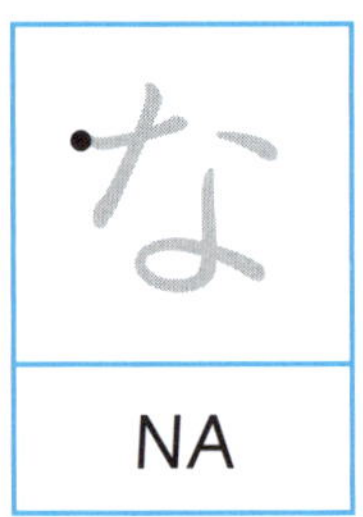

な	に	ぬ	ね	の
NA	NI	NU	NE	NO

Colour in the shapes that have に ぬ or の.

Leave the shapes that have な or ね blank.

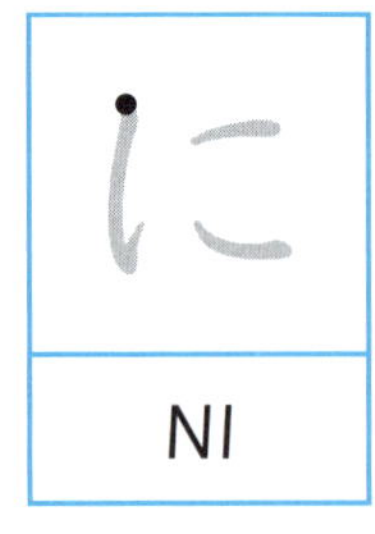

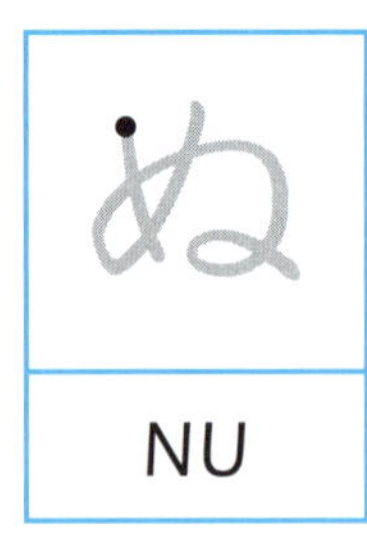

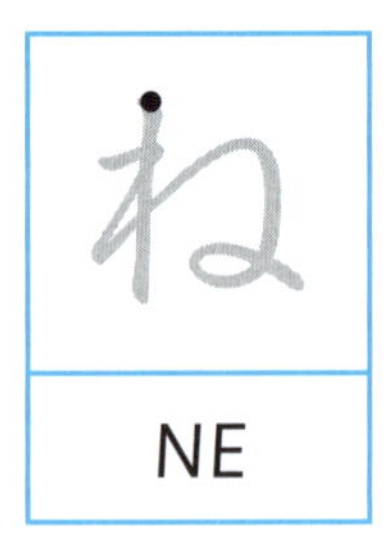

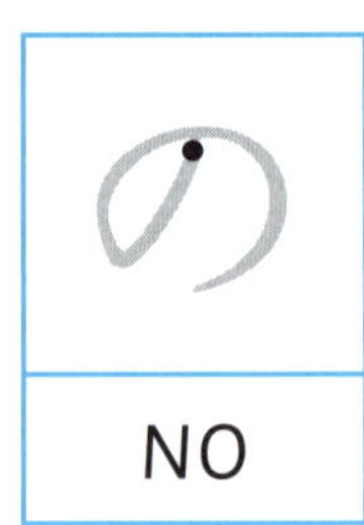

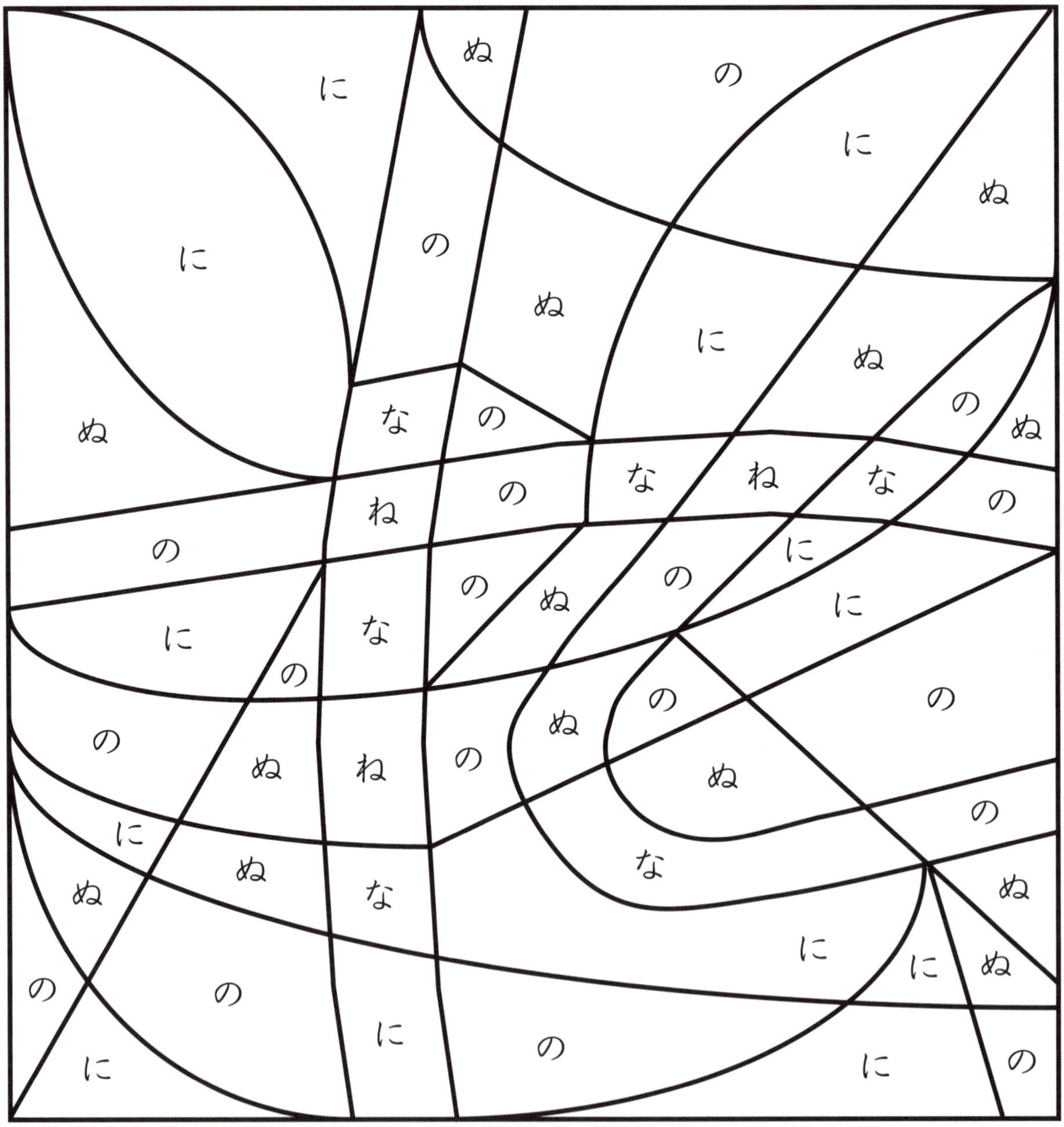

Which hiragana letter was hidden in the picture?

ROMAJI	HIRAGANA

HA	は	は	は	は	は	は	は
HI	ひ	ひ	ひ	ひ	ひ	ひ	ひ
FU	ふ	ふ	ふ	ふ	ふ	ふ	ふ
HE	へ	へ	へ	へ	へ	へ	へ
HO	ほ	ほ	ほ	ほ	ほ	ほ	ほ

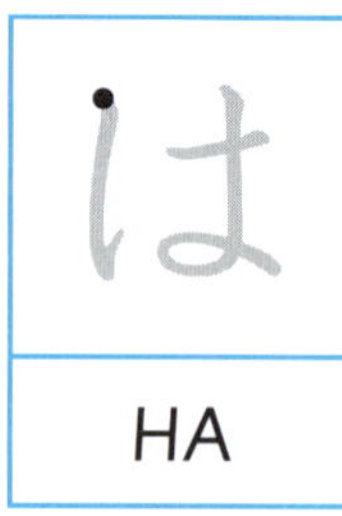

HA

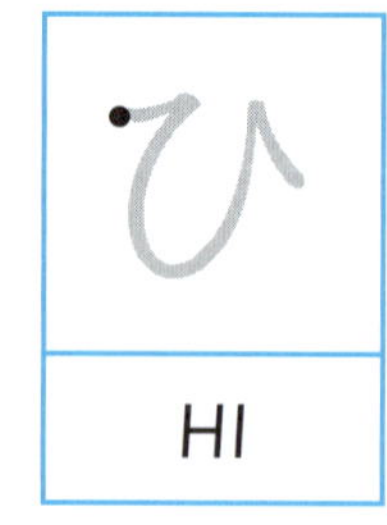

HI

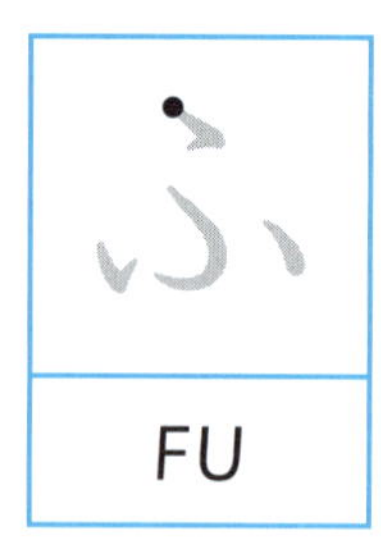

FU

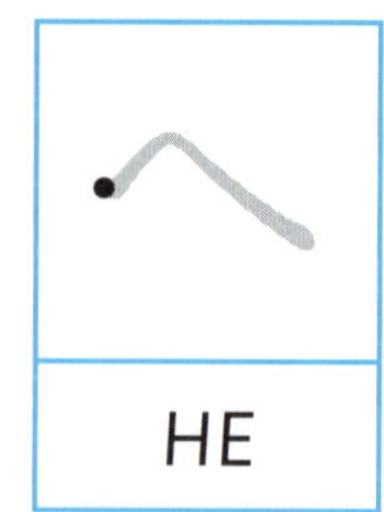

HE

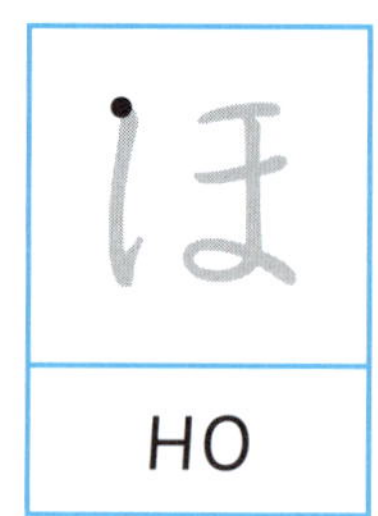

HO

Fill in the missing hiragana letters to complete the labels.

HA	CHI

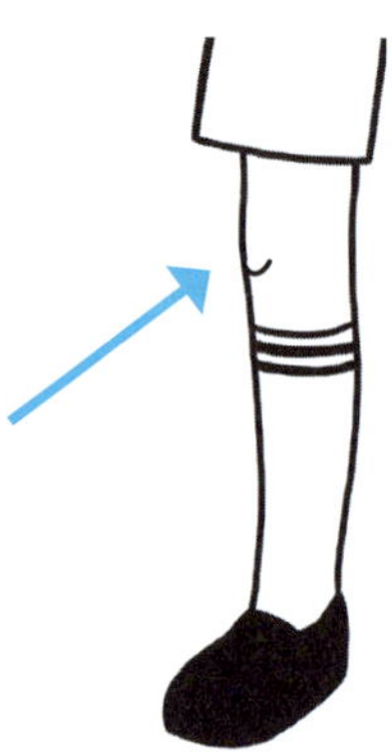

	ざ
HI	ZA

に		ん
NI	HO	N

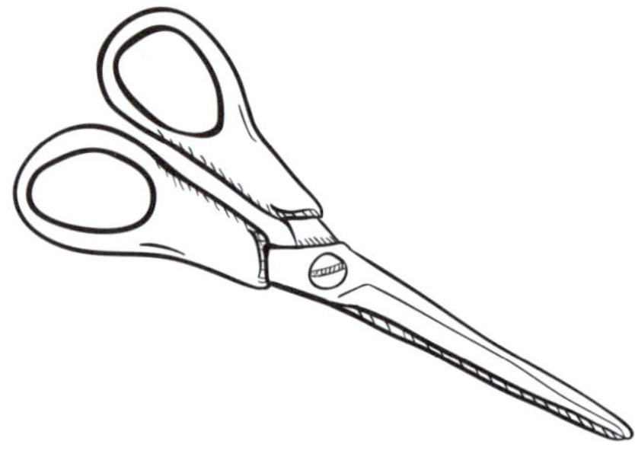

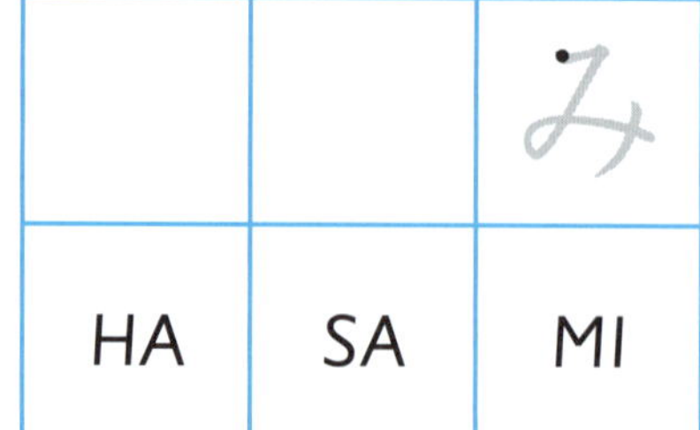

		み
HA	SA	MI

	び
HE	BI

	じ
FU	JI

MA	一	二	ま	ま	ま	ま	ま
MI	み	み	み	み	み	み	み
MU	一	む	む	む	む	む	む
ME	ヽ	め	め	め	め	め	め
MO	し	も	も	も	も	も	も

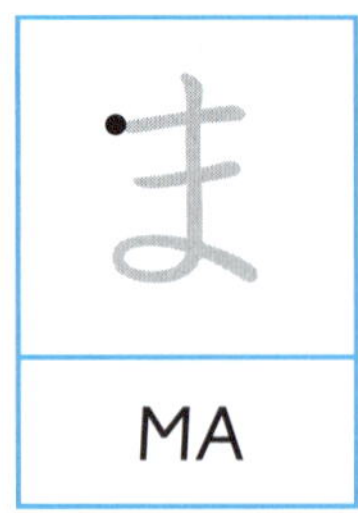

MA

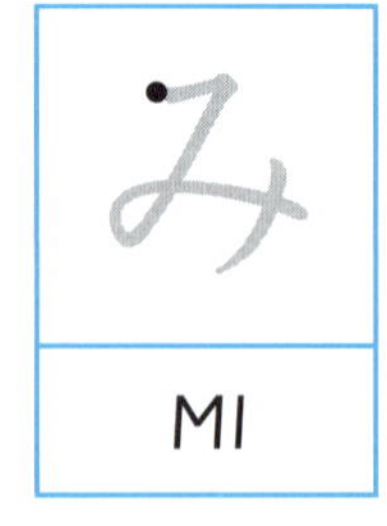

MI

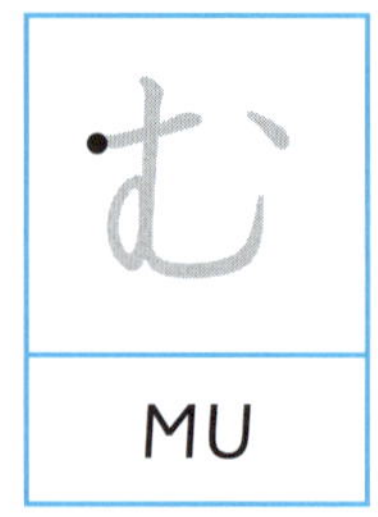

MU

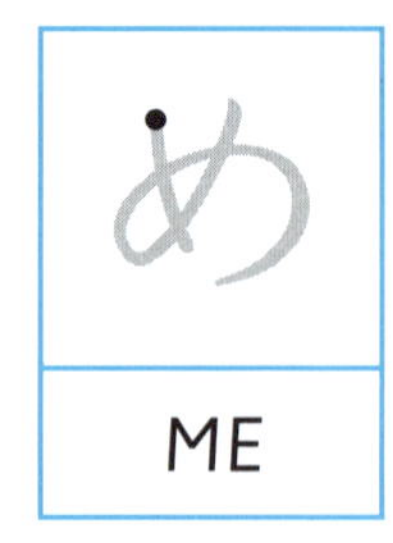

ME

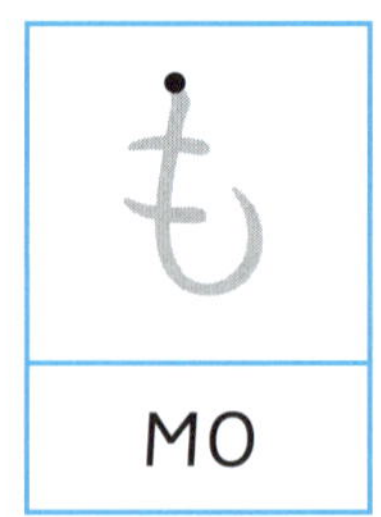

MO

Write the matching hiragana letters in the blank boxes.

MA

MI

MU

ME

MO

YA	つ	う	や	や	や	や	や
YU	い	ゆ	ゆ	ゆ	ゆ	ゆ	ゆ
YO	ˉ	よ	よ	よ	よ	よ	よ

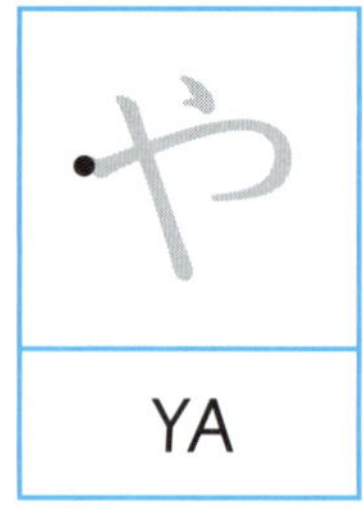

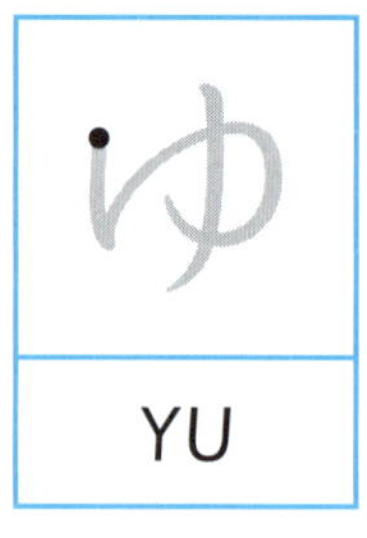

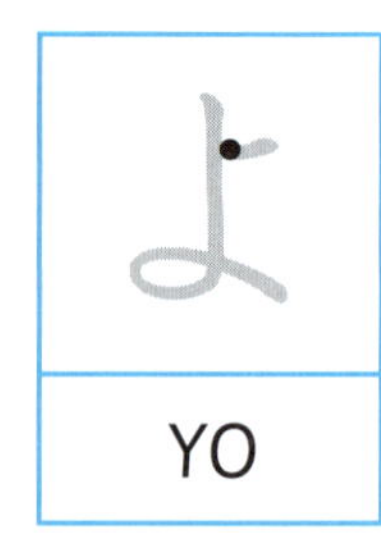

Trace over the correct hiragana letter.

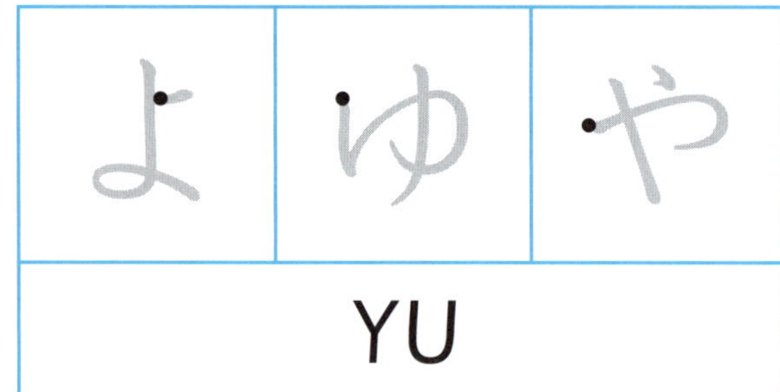

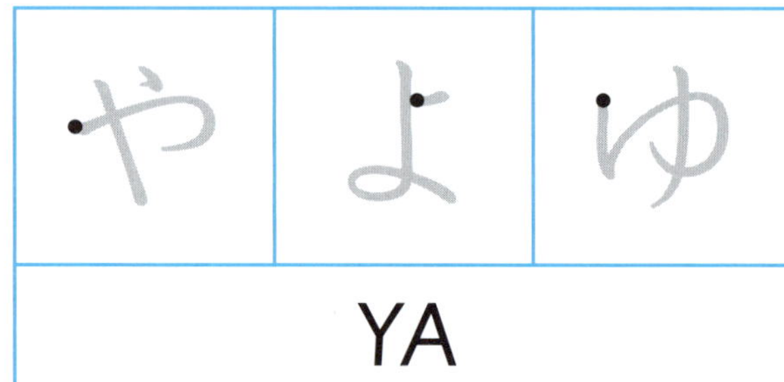

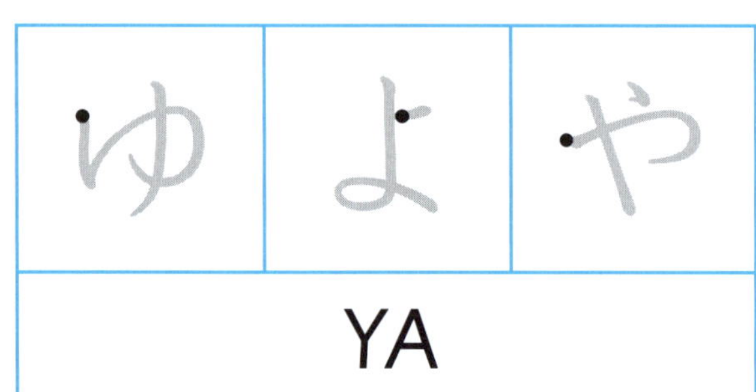

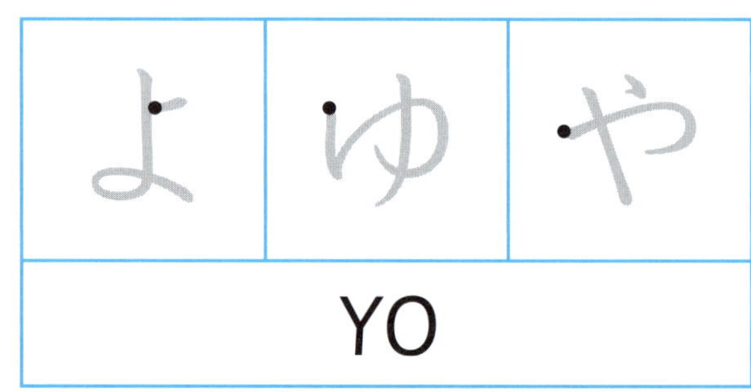

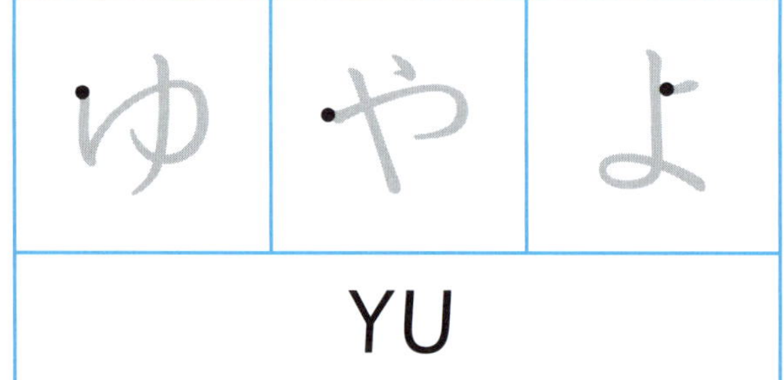

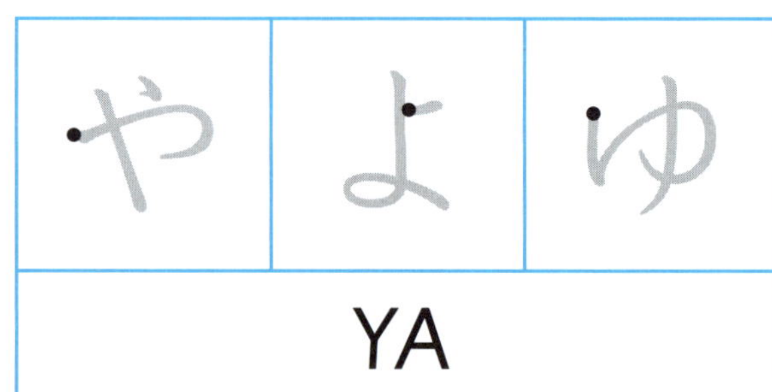

Can you remember these hiragana letters? Trace over them, then write your answers in romaji.

み

ま

そ

RA	ら	ら	ら	ら	ら	ら	ら
RI	り	り	り	り	り	り	り
RU	る	る	る	る	る	る	る
RE	れ	れ	れ	れ	れ	れ	れ
RO	ろ	ろ	ろ	ろ	ろ	ろ	ろ

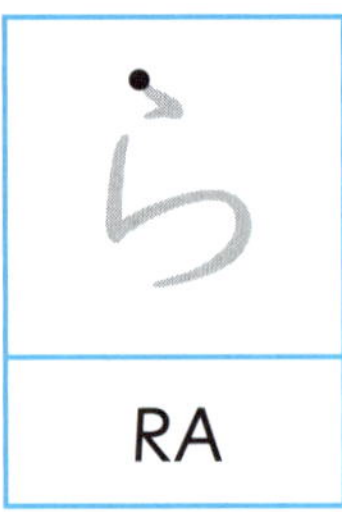	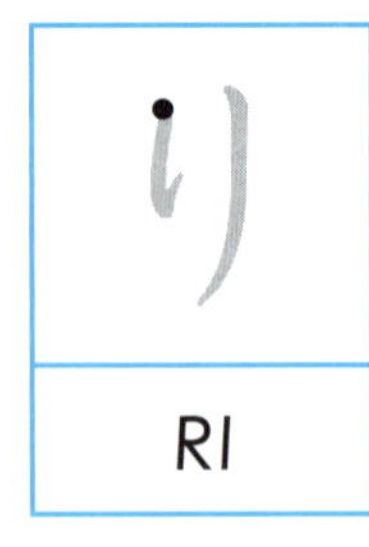		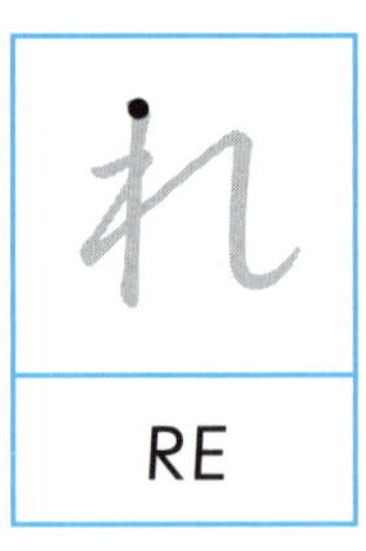	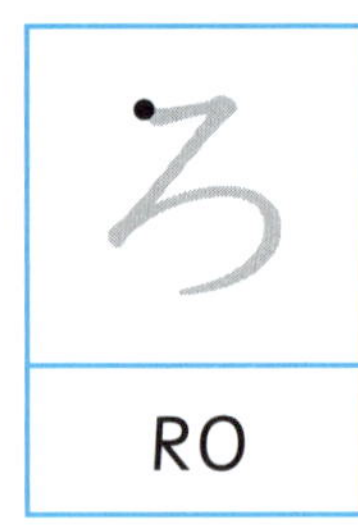
RA	RI	RU	RE	RO

Turn the hiragana letter RA into a picture of anything you like.

WA	丨	わ	わ	わ	わ	わ	わ
particle O	一	ち	を	を	を	を	を
N	ん	ん	ん	ん	ん	ん	ん

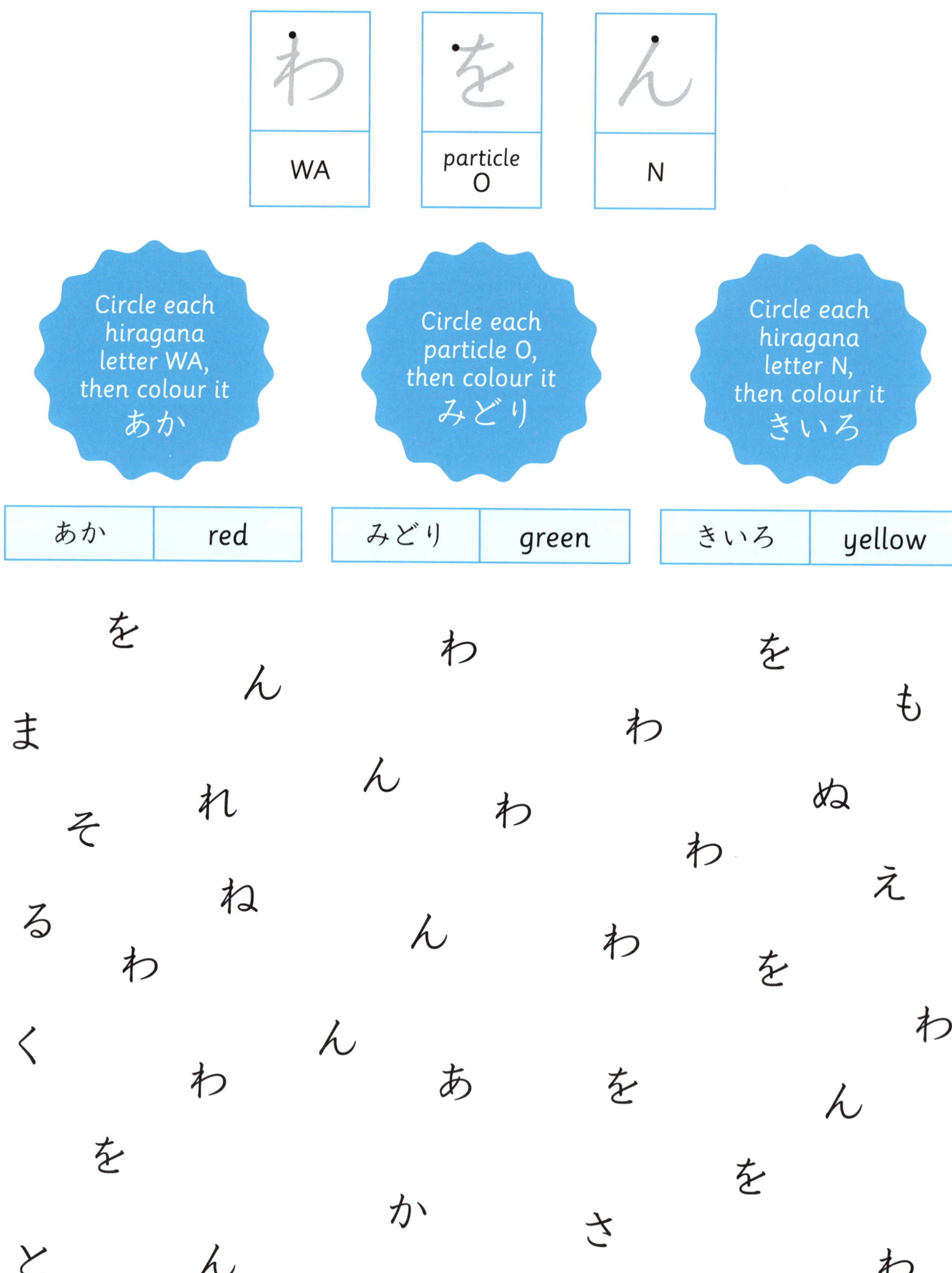
わ
WA
を
particle O
ん
N
Circle each hiragana letter WA, then colour it あか
Circle each particle O, then colour it みどり
Circle each hiragana letter N, then colour it きいろ
あか red
みどり green
きいろ yellow

GA	が
GI	ぎ
GU	ぐ
GE	げ
GO	ご

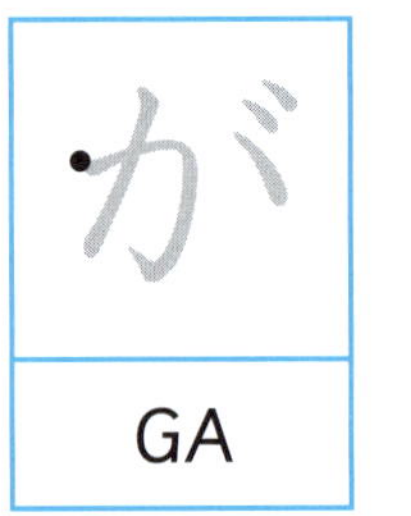

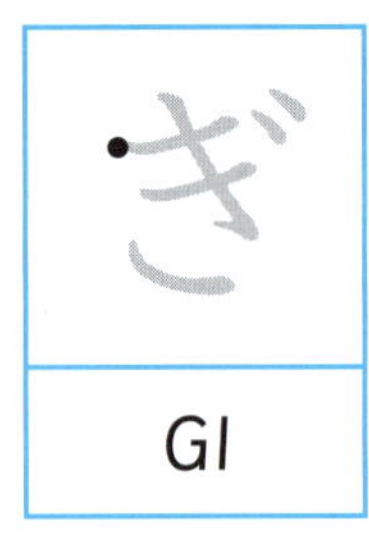

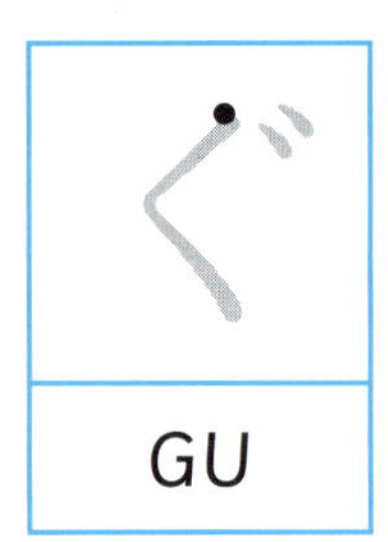

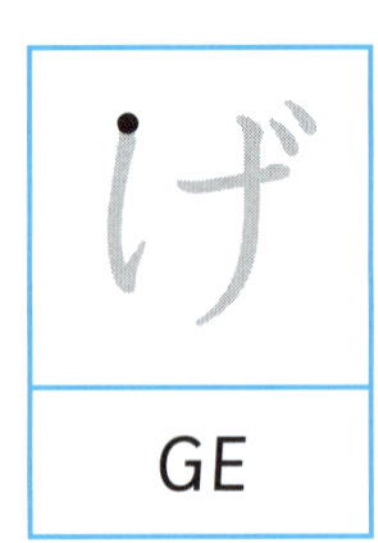

Trace over the correct hiragana letter.

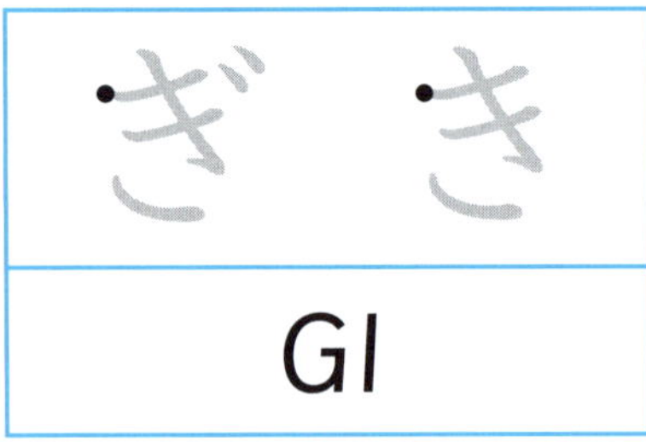

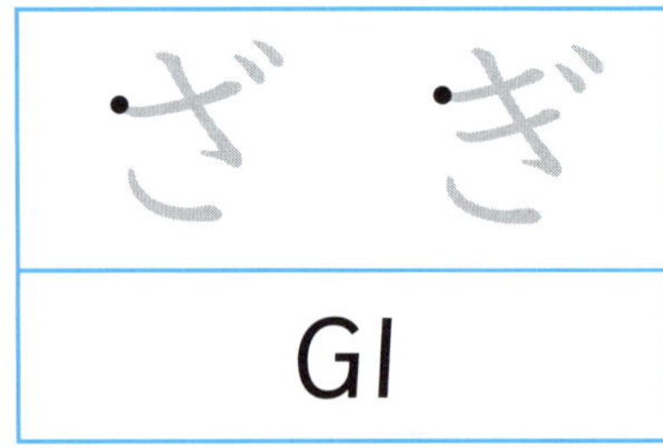

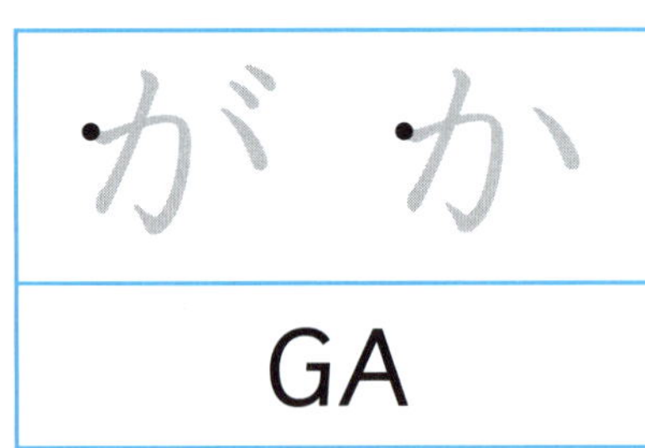

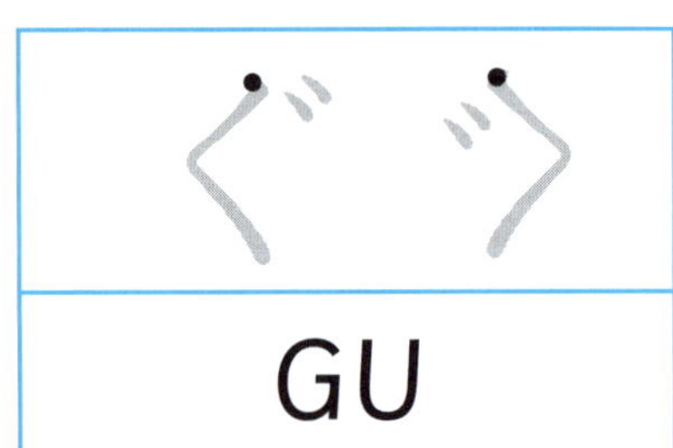

Trace over the hiragana letters, then join them with a line to the matching romaji letters.

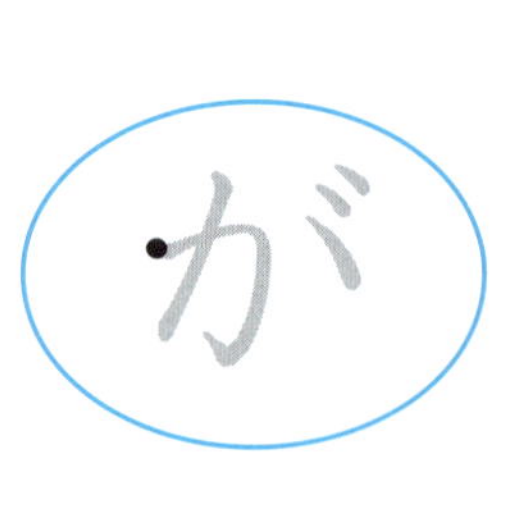

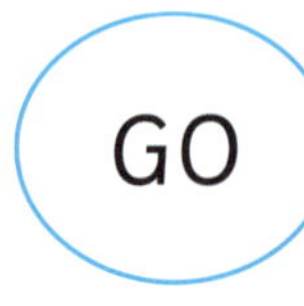

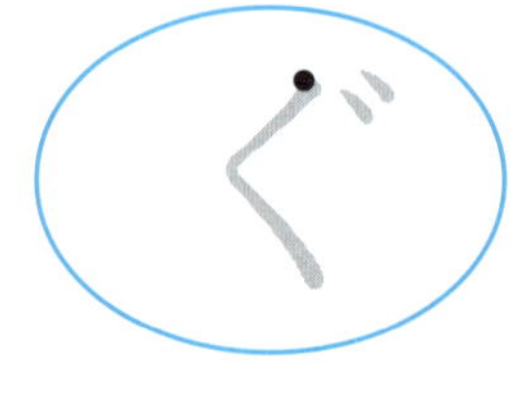

GE

ZA	一	さ	さ	ざ	ざ	ざ	ざ
JI	し	じ	じ	じ	じ	じ	じ
ZU	一	す	ず	ず	ず	ず	ず
ZE	一	十	せ	ぜ	ぜ	ぜ	ぜ
ZO	そ	ぞ	ぞ	ぞ	ぞ	ぞ	ぞ

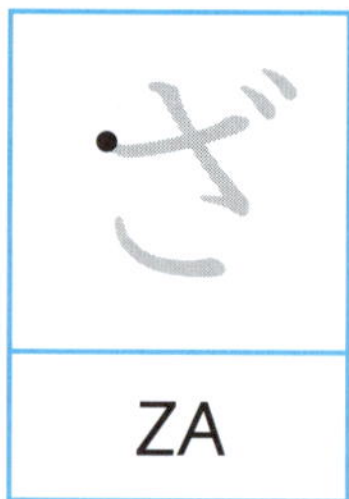

ざ	じ	ず	ぜ	ぞ
ZA	JI	ZU	ZE	ZO

Help the monkey find the hot springs. Trace over the hiragana letters along the correct path.

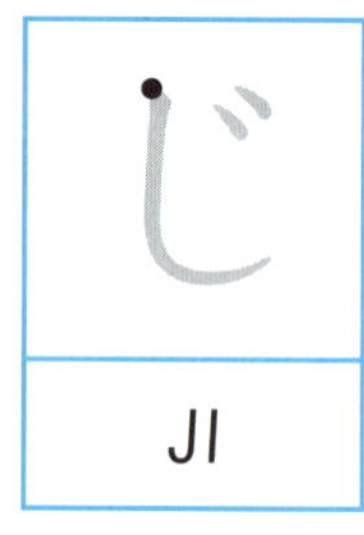

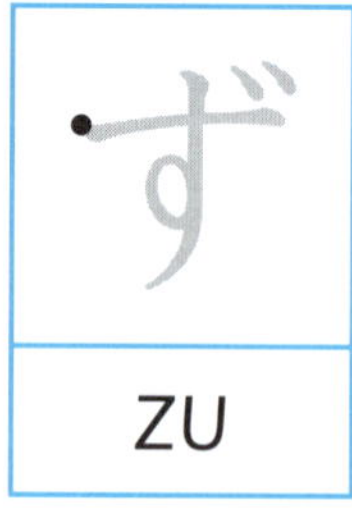

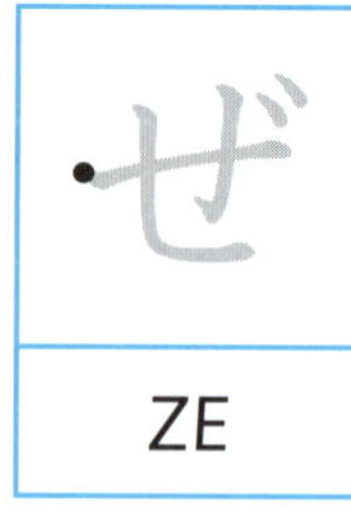

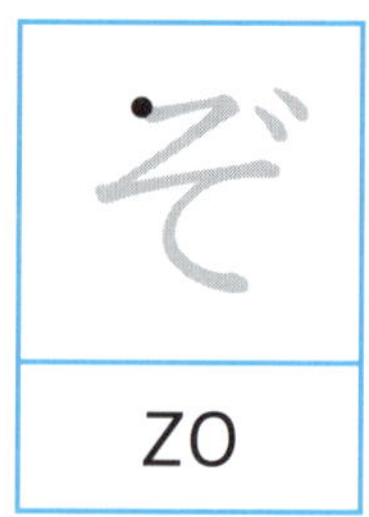

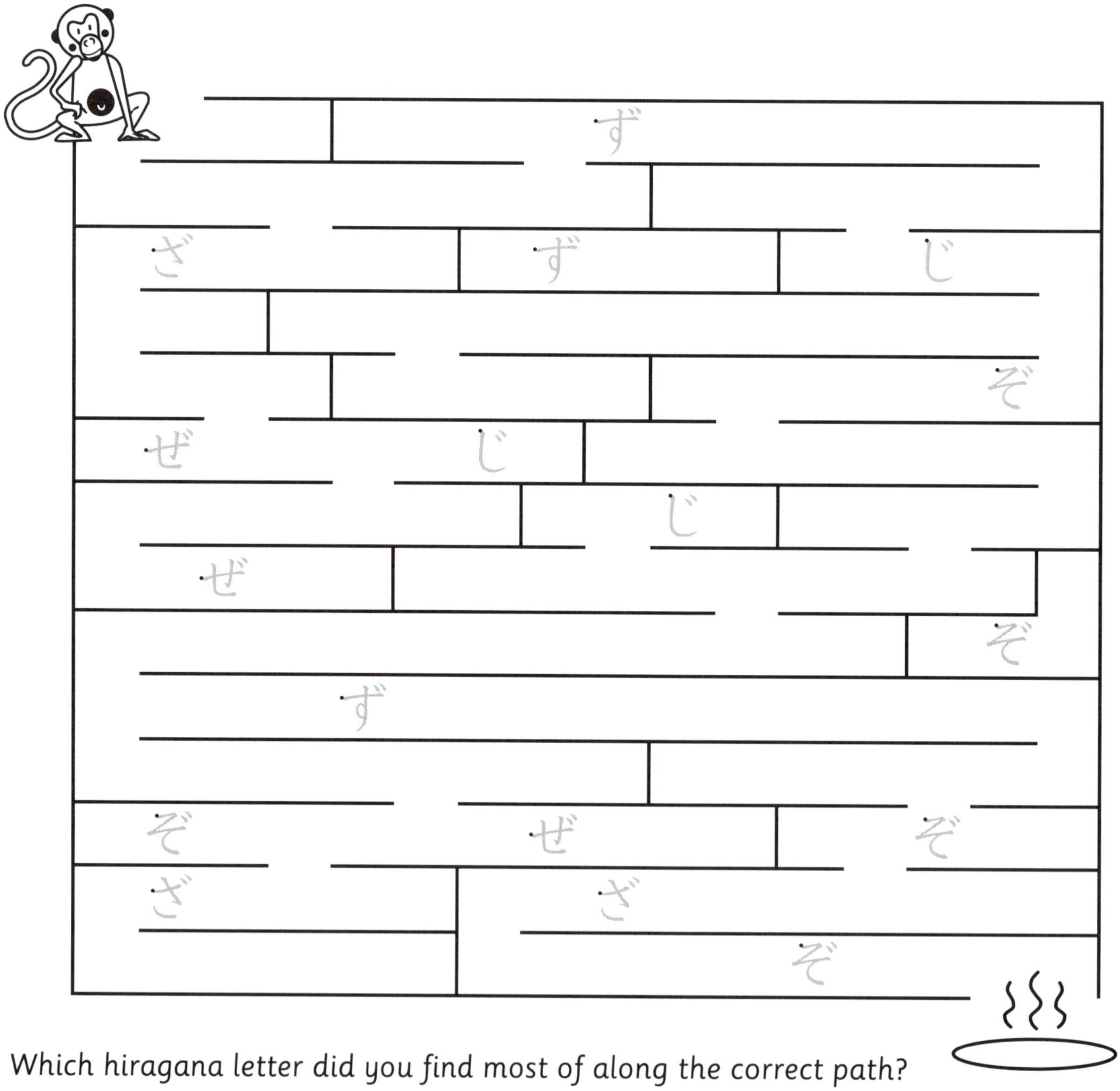

Which hiragana letter did you find most of along the correct path? Insert it in the blank box below to find the mystery word.

	う

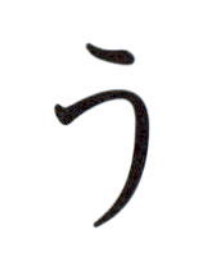

What is the mystery word in English? ____________________

DA	一	ナ	ナ	た	だ	だ	だ
DE	て	で	で	で	で	で	で
DO	ヽ	と	ど	ど	ど	ど	ど

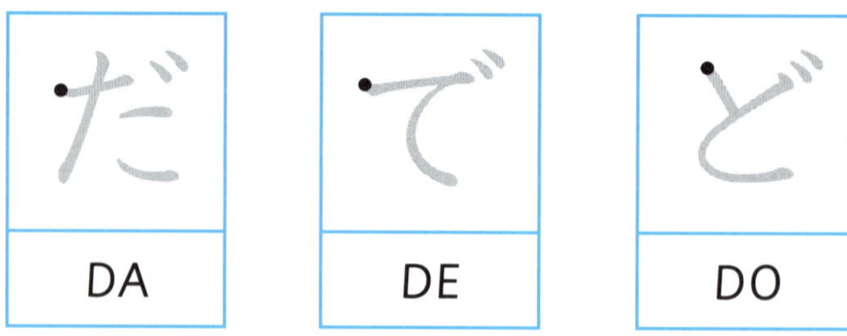

Trace over the correct hiragana letter in each row.

DA	た	と	だ	だ	で	た	だ	ど
DE	で	で	ど	で	て	と	だ	だ
DO	だ	ど	で	ぐ	て	ど	た	と

Add one stroke to complete each hiragana letter.

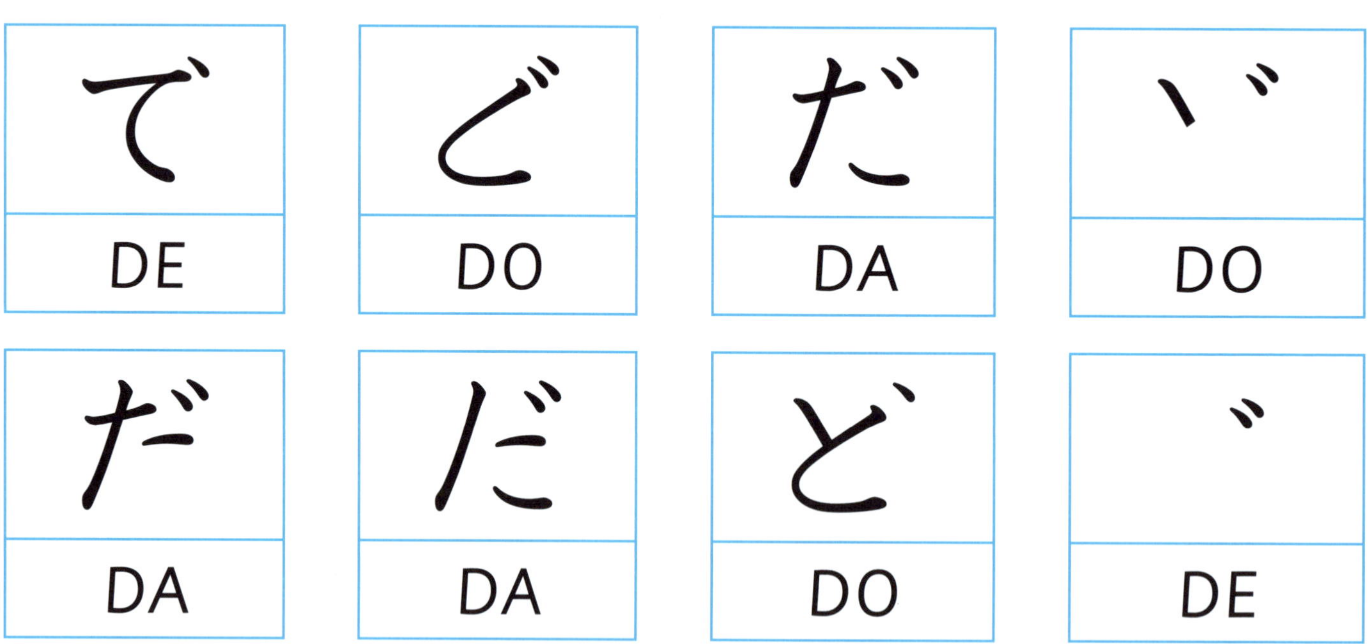

BA			は	ば	ば	ば	ば
BI	ひ	び	び	び	び	び	び
BU			ふ	ふ	ぶ	ぶ	ぶ
BE	へ	べ	べ	べ	べ	べ	べ
BO				ほ	ぼ	ぼ	ぼ

	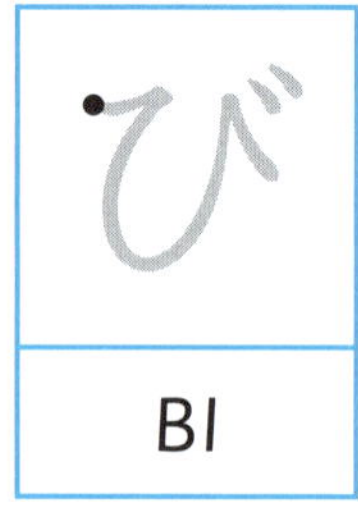	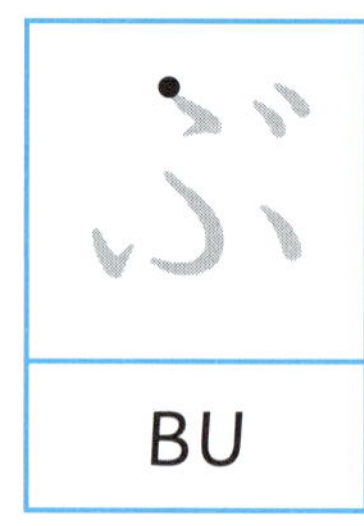	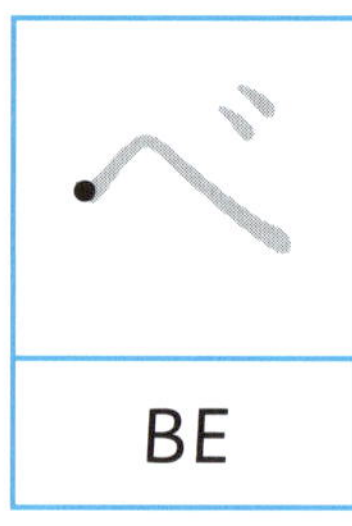	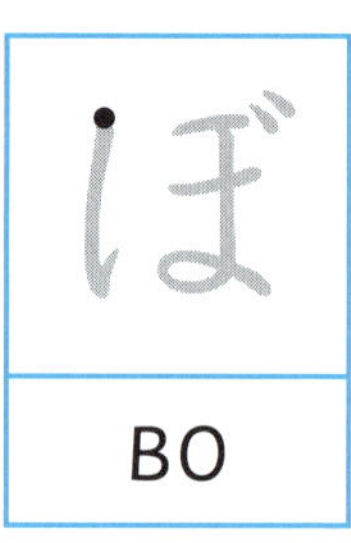
BA	BI	BU	BE	BO

In the first grid, a large BE hiragana letter has been made out of small BE hiragana letters. Trace over the small hiragana letters, then choose three other 'B' hiragana letters to make in the same way in the remaining grids. Label your letters in romaji.

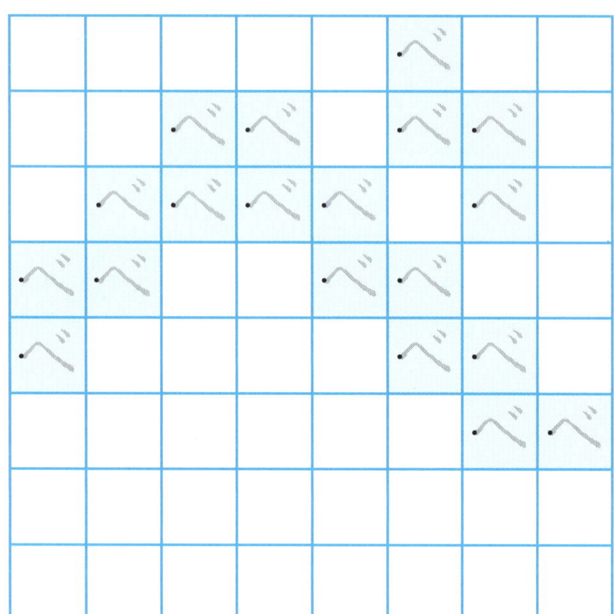

This is the hiragana letter: BE

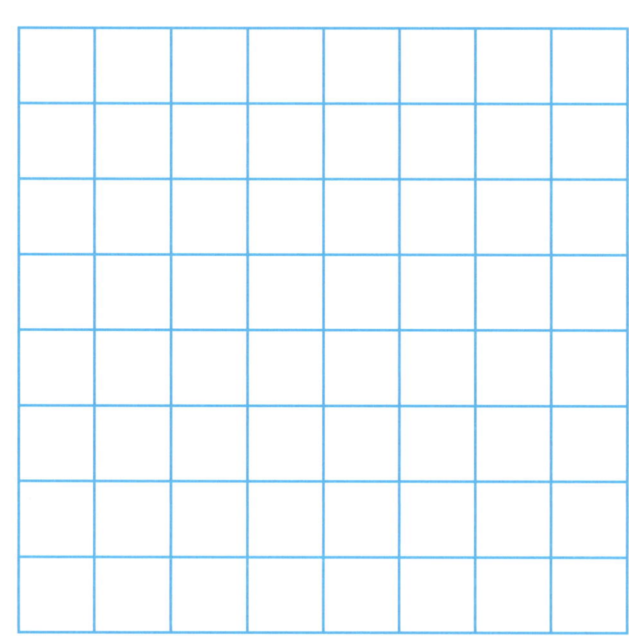

This is the hiragana letter: ________

This is the hiragana letter: ________

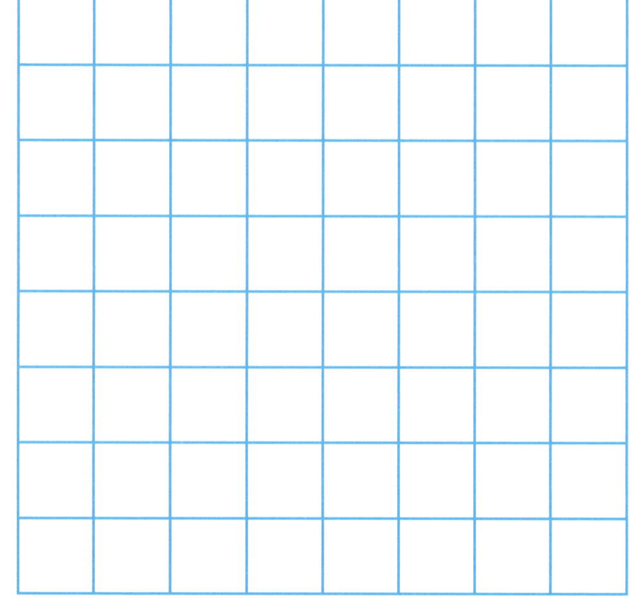

This is the hiragana letter: ________

PA	ぱ
PI	ぴ
PU	ぷ
PE	ぺ
PO	ぽ

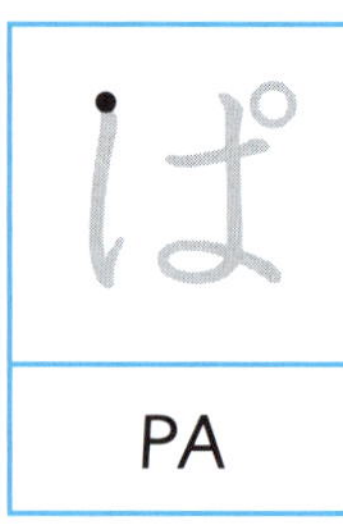	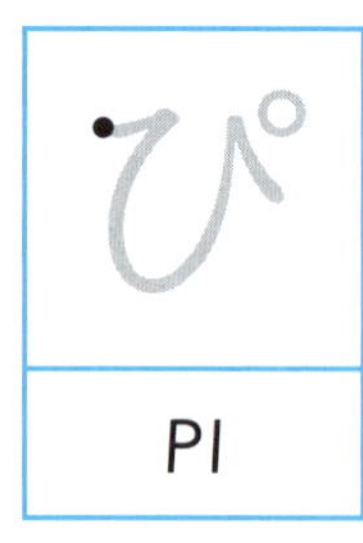	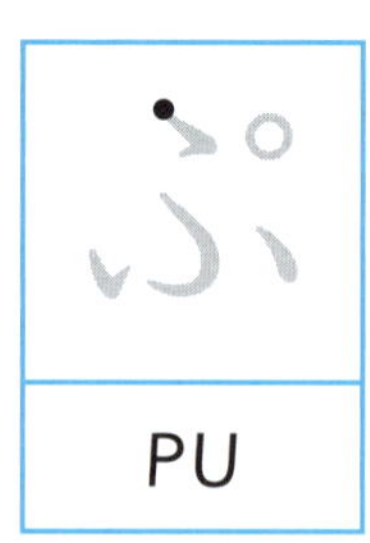	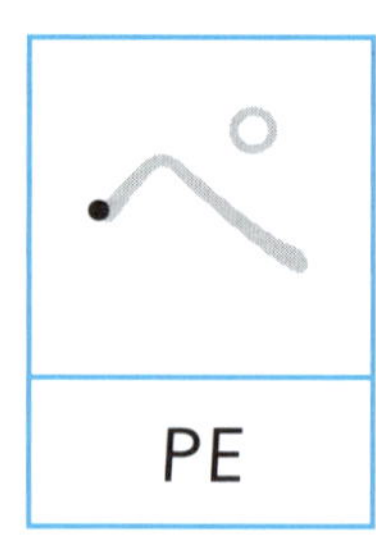	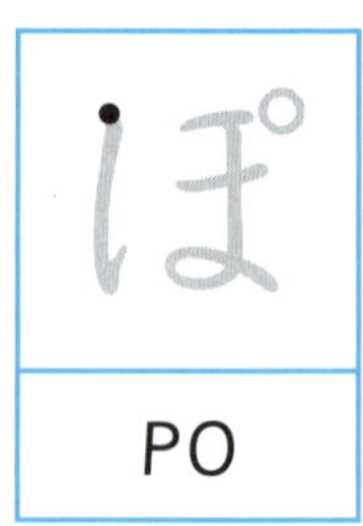
PA	PI	PU	PE	PO

Connect each set of ぱ ぴ ぷ ぺ ぽ hiragana letters in order. Always start with ぱ!

Which hiragana letter was hidden in the picture?

Romaji

Can you remember these hiragana letters? Write them in the blank boxes.

KA		MO		ZO		TE		O	

Trace over ONE word or sentence in each box, then follow your teacher's instructions.

REVISION BINGO		
おおさか ほっかいどう しこく	にほん ほんしゅう とうきょう	さい ねんせい
わたしは KARAです。 三ねんせい です。	ELIJAHくん HANAさん 十さい	ぼく わたし くん
こんにちは ぼくは BRYCEです。	八さい 四ねんせい 九さい	きゅうしゅう です

Trace over ONE letter or number in each box, then follow your teacher's instructions.

REVISION BINGO		
い う お	あ し く	え さ き
十六 十二 十四	七 か 十	て け た
と こ そ	十三 十八 せ	す の ち

Trace over ONE word in each box, then follow your teacher's instructions.

REVISION BINGO		
こんにちは べんきょうします	二十三 二十五 二十八	ちゃいろ くろ グレー
五十 二十四 八十	おおさか とうきょう にほん	むらさき ピンク オレンジ
みどり あか きいろ	八さい です 三ねんせい	たべます よみます みます

Trace over ONE letter or number in each box, then follow your teacher's instructions.

REVISION BINGO		
い う か	く や し	て の ひ
む ぬ ね	み ふ せ	へ 六 ま
え こ な	と そ き	す ち 五

Trace over ONE word or sentence in each box, then follow your teacher's instructions.

REVISION BINGO		
ください ほん にほんご	みどり むらさき きいろ	みてください。 サンドイッチ たべます
べんきょう します ほんを よみます。	よんで ください。 たべて ください。	みます よみます です
四ねんせい 十さいです。 二十七	しろ あお ちゃいろ	テレビ べんきょう してください。

Trace over ONE letter or number in each box, then follow your teacher's instructions.

REVISION BINGO		
と ぬ ね	て め ひ	じ し そ
が 十一 ぞ	い う え	ゆ つ る
す を ぐ	ず げ ち	ご み 四

Trace over ONE word or sentence in each box, then follow your teacher's instructions.

REVISION BINGO		
わたし ぼく です	八じ 十じ 二じ	五じに たべます。 三じによんで ください。
グレー ちゃいろ くろ	みどり あか きいろ	二十九 五十 六十
よんで ください。 よみます	にほん しこく とうきょう	にほんごを べんきょう します。 みます

Trace over ONE hiragana letter in each box, then follow your teacher's instructions.

REVISION BINGO		
と め よ	く ゆ そ	み ち る
で ぬ だ	い こ え	て ぽ れ
す ね べ	ぴ ば ら	わ ず り

LISTENING

Listen to the teacher, then circle the correct answer.

1	2	3	4	5
3 years old	hello	8 years old	I am Taka.	30
grade 5	I am Kara.	40	grade 4	50
I am Bryce.	I'm 9 years old.	grade 3	I'm 7 years old.	60

READING

Look at the cards the teacher will show you. Circle the correct answer.

6	7	8	9	10
TSU	SO	KU	CHI	SU
KA	particle O	I	KE	SE
SHI	KI	TA	SA	KO

Look at the map of Japan. Connect the names of the two main cities and four main islands to the correct parts of the map. Circle the name of the capital city.

Honshu

しこく
Shikoku

おおさか
Osaka

CONGRATULATIONS! You remembered ______ things about Japan and its language.

HOW MUCH CAN YOU REMEMBER? LL 1-8; WL 1-8

LISTENING

Listen to the teacher, then circle the correct answer.

1	2	3	4	5
25 yellow 29	watch/look blue purple	grey pink white	23 29 28	orange red black

6	7	8	9	10
read watch/look learn	50 24 40	green learn 21	grey brown orange	grade 8 80 8 years old

READING

Look at the cards the teacher will show you. Circle the correct answer.

1	2	3	4	5
MA CHI NI	NA FU HA	KU HI MI	NU MU KO	YA HE KI

6	7	8	9	10
TO YU NO	NE TE SHI	SO MO TSU	ME TA SE	HO SU YO

CONGRATULATIONS! You remembered ______ things about Japan and its language.

LISTENING

Listen to the teacher, then circle the correct answer.

1	2	3	4	5
TV Japanese purple	orange red black	brown TV sandwich	book 60 Japanese	green learn read

6	7	8	9	10
read watch/ look Please learn.	Elsa eats. Please eat. Elsa learns.	Please watch/ look. watch/look Please eat.	read a book learn Japanese Please eat.	brown Japanese 8 years old

READING

Look at the cards the teacher will show you. Circle the correct answer.

1	2	3	4	5
particle O CHI NI	NA FU GE	KU GU MI	RO ZO RU	RA HE KI

6	7	8	9	10
TO SA YO	NE WA RI	SO GI TSU	GA JI N	HO YU KA

CONGRATULATIONS! You remembered ______ things about Japan and its language.

LISTENING

Listen to the teacher, then circle the correct answer.

1	2	3	4	5
TV	3 o'clock	please	sandwich	read a book
Japanese	9 o'clock	hello	Japanese	learn Japanese
book	12 o'clock	sandwich	Please eat.	Please eat.

6	7	8	9	10
Please read at 2 o'clock.	I'm in grade 3.	I read at 8 o'clock.	Taka reads.	I am Elsa.
I read at 2 o'clock.	I'm 3 years old.	I read at 7 o'clock.	I eat at 5 o'clock.	Elsa reads a book.
Please learn.	It's 3 o'clock.	Please read.	I read at 5 o'clock.	Elsa reads at 1 o'clock.

READING

Look at the cards the teacher will show you. Circle the correct answer.

1	2	3	4	5
JI	ZE	KU	RO	HE
CHI	particle O	GU	DO	BE
NI	GE	BU	RU	PE

6	7	8	9	10
TO	NE	ZO	GA	PI
DE	WA	GI	TA	YU
YO	PU	TSU	BA	PA

CONGRATULATIONS! You remembered ______ things about Japan and its language.

WORDLIST – ENGLISH/JAPANESE		
English	**Kanji/Hiragana**	**Romaji**
1 · one	一 / いち	I CHI
2 · two	二 / に	NI
3 · three	三 / さん	SA N
4 · four	四 / し / よん	SHI/YO N
5 · five	五 / ご	GO
6 · six	六 / ろく	RO KU
7 · seven	七 / しち / なな	SHI CHI/NA NA
8 · eight	八 / はち	HA CHI
9 · nine	九 / く / きゅう	KU/KYU U
10 · ten	十 / じゅう	JU U
11 · eleven	十一 / じゅう いち	JU U I CHI
12 · twelve	十二 / じゅう に	JU U NI
13 · thirteen	十三 / じゅう さん	JU U SA N
14 · fourteen	十四 / じゅう し / よん	JU U SHI/YO N
15 · fifteen	十五 / じゅう ご	JU U GO
16 · sixteen	十六 / じゅう ろく	JU U RO KU
17 · seventeen	十七 / じゅう しち / なな	JU U SHI CHI/NA NA
18 · eighteen	十八 / じゅう はち	JU U HA CHI
19 · nineteen	十九 / じゅう く / きゅう	JU U KU/KYU U
20 · twenty	二十 / にじゅう	NI JU U
21 · twenty-one	二十一 / にじゅう いち	NI JU U I CHI
22 · twenty-two	二十二 / にじゅう に	NI JU U NI
23 · twenty-three	二十三 / にじゅう さん	NI JU U SA N
24 · twenty-four	二十四 / にじゅう し / よん	NI JU U SHI/YO N
25 · twenty-five	二十五 / にじゅう ご	NI JU U GO
26 · twenty-six	二十六 / にじゅう ろく	NI JU U RO KU
27 · twenty-seven	二十七 / にじゅう しち / なな	NI JU U SHI CHI/NA NA
28 · twenty-eight	二十八 / にじゅう はち	NI JU U HA CHI
29 · twenty-nine	二十九 / にじゅう く / きゅう	NI JU U KU/KYU U
30 · thirty	三十 / さん じゅう	SA N JU U
40 · forty	四十 / よん じゅう	YO N JU U
50 · fifty	五十 / ご じゅう	GO JU U
60 · sixty	六十 / ろく じゅう	RO KU JU U
70 · seventy	七十 / しち / なな じゅう	SHI CHI/NA NA JU U
80 · eighty	八十 / はち じゅう	HA CHI JU U
90 · ninety	九十 / きゅう じゅう	KYU U JU U

WORDLIST – ENGLISH/JAPANESE		
English	**Kanji/Hiragana/Katakana**	**Romaji**
1 o'clock	一じ / いちじ	I CHI JI
2 o'clock	二じ / にじ	NI JI
3 o'clock	三じ / さんじ	SA N JI
4 o'clock	四じ / よじ	YO JI
5 o'clock	五じ / ごじ	GO JI
6 o'clock	六じ / ろくじ	RO KU JI
7 o'clock	七じ / しちじ	SHI CHI JI
8 o'clock	八じ / はちじ	HA CHI JI
9 o'clock	九じ / くじ	KU JI
10 o'clock	十じ / じゅうじ	JU U JI
11 o'clock	十一じ / じゅういちじ	JU U I CHI JI
12 o'clock	十二じ / じゅうにじ	JU U NI JI
at (used with time)	に	NI
black	くろ	KU RO
blue	あお	A O
book	ほん	HO N
brown	ちゃいろ	CHA I RO
eat	たべます	TA BE MA SU
green	みどり	MI DO RI
grey	グレー	GU RE E
hello (good day)	こんにちは	KO N NI CHI WA
Hokkaido	ほっかいどう	HO KKA I DO U
Honshu	ほんしゅう	HO N SHU U
I am in grade ...	... ねんせいです。	NE N SE I DE SU
I am ... (used by boys)	ぼく は ... です。	BO KU WA ... DE SU
I am ... (used by girls)	わたし は ... です。	WA TA SHI WA ... DE SU
I am ... years old	... さいです。	... SA I DE SU
Japan	にほん	NI HO N
Japanese	にほんご	NI HO N GO
Kyushu	きゅうしゅう	KYU U SHU U
learn	べんきょう します	BE N KYO U SHI MA SU
o'clock	じ	JI
orange	オレンジ	O RE N JI
Osaka	おおさか	O O SA KA

WORDLIST – ENGLISH/JAPANESE		
English	Hiragana/Katakana	Romaji
particle o	を	O
particle wa	は	WA
pink	ピンク	PI N KU
Please eat.	たべて ください。	TA BE TE KU DA SA I
Please learn.	べんきょう して ください。	BE N KYO U SHI TE KU DA SA I
Please read.	よんで ください。	YO N DE KU DA SA I
Please watch/look.	みて ください。	MI TE KU DA SA I
purple	むらさき	MU RA SA KI
read	よみます	YO MI MA SU
red	あか	A KA
sandwich	サンドイッチ	SA N DO I T CHI
Shikoku	しこく	SHI KO KU
Tokyo	とうきょう	TO U KYO U
TV	テレビ	TE RE BI
used after a boy's name	くん	KU N
used after a girl's name	さん	SA N
watch/look	みます	MI MA SU
What's the time?	いま なんじ です か	I MA NA N JI DE SU KA
white	しろ	SHI RO
yellow	きいろ	KI I RO

HIRAGANA CHART

あ A	い I	う U	え E	お O
か KA	き KI	く KU	け KE	こ KO
が GA	ぎ GI	ぐ GU	げ GE	ご GO
さ SA	し SHI	す SU	せ SE	そ SO
ざ ZA	じ JI	ず ZU	ぜ ZE	ぞ ZO
た TA	ち CHI	つ TSU	て TE	と TO
だ DA			で DE	ど DO
な NA	に NI	ぬ NU	ね NE	の NO
は HA	ひ HI	ふ FU	へ HE	ほ HO
ば BA	び BI	ぶ BU	べ BE	ぼ BO
ぱ PA	ぴ PI	ぷ PU	ぺ PE	ぽ PO
ま MA	み MI	む MU	め ME	も MO
や YA		ゆ YU		よ YO
ら RA	り RI	る RU	れ RE	ろ RO
わ WA				を O
ん N				

HIRAGANA COMBINATION CHART

きゃ	きゅ	きょ
kya	kyu	kyo
ぎゃ	ぎゅ	ぎょ
gya	gyu	gyo
しゃ	しゅ	しょ
sha	shu	sho
じゃ	じゅ	じょ
ja	ju	jo
ちゃ	ちゅ	ちょ
cha	chu	cho
にゃ	にゅ	にょ
nya	nyu	nyo
ひゃ	ひゅ	ひょ
hya	hyu	hyo
びゃ	びゅ	びょ
bya	byu	byo
ぴゃ	ぴゅ	ぴょ
pya	pyu	pyo
みゃ	みゅ	みょ
mya	myu	myo
りゃ	りゅ	りょ
rya	ryu	ryo